For Sue Stubbs and Barry Goldstein
who have made this, and every other
Fearless Critic book, possible

Other books from Robin Goldstein and Fearless Critic Media

Fearless Critic Portland Restaurant Guide

Fearless Critic Houston Restaurant Guide

Fearless Critic Austin Restaurant Guide

Fearless Critic Washington DC Restaurant Guide

Fearless Critic New Haven Restaurant Guide

The Menu: Restaurant Guide to Northampton, Amherst, and the Five-College Area

On fearlesscritic.com

For everyone: restaurant guide content including sortable lists and ratings, what's open now, new reviews, daily rotating reviews, and more

For subscribers: the entire text of Fearless Critic restaurant guides

THE WINE TRIALS 2010

A Fearless Critic book

Second edition, 2010

Printed in the United States of America

ISBN 978-1-6081600-7-5

10 9 8 7 6 5 4 3 2 1

Authors

Robin Goldstein is the founder and editor-in-chief of the Fearless Critic series. He has authored six books of restaurant reviews and has written for more than 30 *Fodor's* travel guides, from Italy to Thailand, Argentina to Hong Kong. Robin is a graduate of Harvard University and the Yale Law School. He has a certificate in cooking from the French Culinary Institute in New York and a WSET advanced wine and spirits certificate.

Alexis Herschkowitsch is a co-author of five Fearless Critic restaurant guides. Alexis has written for the *Fodor's* travel guides to Mexico, Central America, and Thailand. She is a graduate of the University of Texas at Austin, and has a WSET advanced wine and spirits certificate.

Associate Editors

Tyce Walters, who created this edition's wine reviews from the notes of our editorial tasting panel, is a graduate of Yale University, where he founded the wine journal *Vino/Veritas: The Yale Wino*. He has also worked as a wine retail consultant and served as editor of the *Yale Philosophy Review*.

Andrea Armeni has practiced wine law in Napa Valley, taught sustainable development to oenologists in Paris, and currently lives in San Francisco, where he is a reporter for *Emerging Markets* magazine. Andrea is a graduate of Columbia University and the Yale Law School, and has contributed to numerous Fearless Critic food and wine books.

Editorial and blind tasting board

The following people, listed alphabetically, served on our 2010 tasting panels and/or as editorial advisers. The opinions set forth in this book do not necessarily reflect the views of any of these individuals or their affiliated institutions. Any errors are ours alone.

Ellisa Cooper is director of education for Barter House Wine Imports. **Nat Davis**, a member of the American Sommelier Association, has served as the wine director for Uchi restaurant in Austin, Texas. **Brian DiMarco** is owner and president of Barter House Wine Imports and a graduate of the French Culinary Institute in New York City. **Julian Faulkner**, owner and winemaker of Le Grand Cros and Jules Wines in the Côtes de Provence region, has a master's degree in oenology from the École Nationale d'Ingénieurs des Travaux Agricoles de Bordeaux. **Jake Katz** has a WSET advanced wine and spirits certificate, has worked as a statistician at Lehman Brothers, and is a co-author of the article "Do More Expensive Wines Taste Better?". **Karen Man** is a graduate of the French Pastry School in Chicago and cooks at the French Laundry restaurant in Yountville, California. **Erin McReynolds** is managing editor of the Fearless Critic Restaurant Guides, directing a national network of food critics and editing the series. She has also worked in the restaurant industry for more than a decade. **James Morrison** has been beverage director for the Fireman Hospitality Group and is currently a consultant for Barter House Wine Imports. **Stew Navarre** is a graduate of the Culinary Institute of America and has cooked at the Grove restaurant in Houston, Texas. **Benjamin Rosenblum** is an architect based in Berkeley, California, and has contributed to the *Fearless Critic New Haven Restaurant Guide*. **Karl Storchmann** is vice president of the American Association of Wine Economists, managing editor of the Journal of Wine Economics, and associate professor of economics at New York University. **Kent Wang** has been a staff member at the eGullet Society for Culinary Arts & Letters and has contributed to the *Fearless Critic Austin Restaurant Guide*. **Justin Yu** is a graduate of the Culinary Institute of America, has contributed to several Fearless Critic restaurant guides, and currently cooks at Ubuntu restaurant in Napa, California.

Scientific advisory board

The following professors and scientists, listed alphabetically, offered their expertise to help interpret our results and review our methods and conclusions for scientific accuracy. The opinions set forth in this book do not necessarily reflect the views of any of these individuals or their affiliated institutions. Any errors are ours alone.

Anna Dreber Almenberg*, Institute for Financial Research, Stockholm, and the Women and Public Policy Program, Kennedy School of Government, Harvard University

Johan Almenberg*, Ministry of Finance, Sweden

Jacopo Anselmi, Department of Statistics, Yale University

Nathaniel Baum-Snow, Department of Economics, Brown University

Ryan Bradley, University of California, San Francisco Medical Center

Daniela Cammack, Department of Government, Harvard University

Zoe Chance, Harvard Business School

David Eagleman, Department of Neuroscience, Baylor College of Medicine

Jay Emerson*, Department of Statistics, Yale University

Shane Frederick, Sloan School of Management, Massachusetts Institute of Technology

Richard Friberg, Stockholm School of Economics

David Grewal, Department of Government, Harvard University

Erik Grönqvist, Institute of Labour Market Policy Evaluation

Magnus Johannesson, Stockholm School of Economics

Thomas Pfeiffer, Program for Evolutionary Dynamics, Harvard University

Natalia Ramondo, Department of Economics, University of Texas at Austin

Tatiana Schnur, Department of Psychology, Rice University

* Co-authors of the paper "Do More Expensive Wines Taste Better?", which forms the theoretical framework for this book.

Other contributors

The following people contributed generously to our project in numerous ways: organizing or hosting blind tastings, reviewing our methodology and conclusions, editing and proofreading drafts of the manuscript, and even hosting the authors in their homes. The opinions set forth in this book do not necessarily reflect the views of any of these individuals or their affiliated institutions. Any errors are ours alone.

Margarita Barcenas, Event Coordinator
Leah Barton, Event Coordinator
Hal Bayless, Event Coordinator
Nikia Bergan, General Contributor
Adam Brackman, Photographer
Bill Collins, Event Host
Daniel Frommer, General Contributor
James Frutkin, Contributing Editor
Andrew Gajkowski, General Contributor
Navid Ghedami, Event Host
Barry Goldstein, Contributing Editor and Event Host
Rosie Goldstein, Event Host
Kacie Gonzalez, Publishing Assistant
David Grossman, Chef
Claudio Guerra, Event Host
Daniel Horwitz, Contributing Editor and Event Host
Bobby Huegel, Mixologist
Roy Ip, Chef and Event Host
Winnie Ip, Event Host
Jeff Kaplan, Event Coordinator
Anat Kaufman, Photographer
David Kim, Event Coordinator
Sidney Kwiram, Contributing Editor
Duncan Levin, Contributing Editor
Benjamin Lima, Contributing Editor
Josh Loving, Event Host
Rebecca Markovits, Contributing Editor
Beth Martinez, Event Host
Dan Martinez, Event Host

Other contributors *continued*

Charles Mayes, Event Host
Colin McCarthy, Event Coordinator
Caroline McLean, Event Host
David Menschel, Contributing Editor
Clare Murumba, Event Host
Angie Niles, Event Coordinator
Justin Nowell, Video Editor
Brane Poledica, Event Host
Isaure de Pontbriand, Contributing Editor
Karisa Prestera, Event Host
Daniel Rosenblum, Photographer
Abigail Roth, Event Coordinator
James Saccento, General Contributor
Marcus Samuelsson, Chef and Event Host
Claude Solliard, Chef and Event Host
Kelly Stecker, Publishing Assistant and Photographer
Brian Stubbs, Event Host
Harold Stubbs, Contributing Editor
Lu Stubbs, Contributing Editor
Susan Stubbs, Contributing Editor and Event Host
Cody Taylor, Event Coordinator
Mark Trachtenberg, Event Host
Darya Trapeznikova, Event Coordinator
Andy Vickery, Event Host
Carol Vickery, Event Host

We would also like to thank the following restaurants for hosting events and wine tastings for *The Wine Trials*:

Aquavit, New York, NY
Bella's, New York, NY
Bistro Lancaster, Houston, TX
Bistro Les Gras, Northampton, MA
Café Josie, Austin, TX
Fino, Austin, TX

Paradise City Tavern, Northampton, MA
Le Petit Café, Branford, CT
Lotus, New York, NY
Seppi's, New York, NY
Upstairs on the Square, Cambridge, MA

Experimental blind tasters

The following people participated in the 2008 blind-tasting experiment that formed the empirical basis for the paper "Do More Expensive Wines Taste Better?" and the framework for the first portion of this book. The opinions set forth in this book do not necessarily reflect the views of any of these individuals. Any errors are ours alone.

Suzanne Adelman, Caroline Adler, Bob Agoglia, Ali Ahsan, Frances Aldous-Worley, Elnaz Alipour-Assiabi, Johan Almenberg, Anna Dreber Almenberg, Michael Amendola, Janelle Anderson, Whitney Angstadt, Lorenzo Aragona, Fernando Aramburo, Larinia Arena, Brenda Audino, Laura Austin, Marty Austin, Leila Ayachi, Leigh M. Bailey, Donna L. Balin, Scott A. Balin, David Ball, Nicole Ball, Oleg Balter, Shai Bandner, Margarita Barcenas, Rhondale-Marie Barras, Catherine Barry, Leah Barton, Ben Batchelder, Anne C. Bauer, Nathaniel Baum-Snow, Hal Bayless, Andrew Benner, Zachary Bennett, Steven Bercu, Amber Berend, Edward H. Berman, Julia Berman, Jason Berns, Jennifer Berns, Susan Biancani, Chris Black, J.D. Bloodworth, Rayna Bourke, Vanessa Treviño Boyd, Wood Boyles, Adam Brackman, Uda M. Bradford, Delana Brandon, Benjamin J. Brandow, Kevin Brass, Lietza Brass, Judith Brock, Patrick Brock, Stacey Brock, Aileen B. Brophy, Ezra T. Brown, Jaclynn T. Brown, Joy Brunner, L.R. Brunner, S.S. Brunner, Robert Buchele, Thomas Burke, Gary L. Bush, Nancy H. Bush, Matthew J. Caballero, Mark Cabell, Rick Cagney, Michele Camp, Jeff Caplan, Lisa Carley, Ale Carlos, Robert Carroll, Kimberly Casey, Marlon Castillo, Claire Champagne, John Champagne, Zoe Chance, Benjamin Chang, Helen Chong, Gaetan Ciampini, Dennis Clark, John B. Clutterbuck, Suzanna Cole, William M. Collins, Marcus Allen Cooper, Russell W. Cooper, David Cordúa, Denis Costaz, Nadia Croes, Katy Cuddihee, Marc Cuenod, Martha Cuenod, Nat Davis, C.J. Dean, Frank Debons, Jana Demetral, Nisha Desai, Brian DiMarco, Shoshana Dobrow, Chezmin N. Dolinsky, Susan K. Dudek, Shaun Duffy, Carol Duke, Seth Dunn, Kenneth Dyer, Julie Sinclair Eakin, James Endicott, Joel Ephross, Matt Epstein, Sarah Escobar, Samantha Essen, Julie Fairbanks, Virginia H. Fallon, Julian Faulkner, Amy E. Ferrer, Monica Fields, Ben Fieman, Cristina Finan, Paul Flores, Sharla Flores,

Experimental blind tasters *continued*

Christine Folch, Eric Foret, Ana Fox, Judd Frankel, Shane Frederick, John Freeman, Sylvia Freeman, Morgan Friedman, Marika Frumes, Jim Frutkin, Eleni Gage, Andrew Gajkowski, Jessica L. Gant, Seanna Garrison, Thomas J. Garza, Marva Gay, Robert Gerstle, Jeffrey Giles, Julie Goldman, Barry Goldstein, Maria J. Gomez, Nick Gossett, Michelle Grasso, Ed Greenbaum, Claire Liu Greenberg, Seth Grossman, Frederic Guarino, Elaine Gubbins, Megan G. Gubbins, Claudio Guerra, Elisabeth Gutowski, John Ha, Casey Dué Hackney, Ryan Hackney, Lauren Hale, Deb Hall, William Erin Hall, Mike Handel, Tracie Handel, Michelle S. Hardy, Joan Harmon, Amy K. Harper, Elizabeth W. Harries, Brian Hay, Monica Hayes, Kristen Hendricks, Jodie Hermann, David Hesse, Leslie Hill, Ed Hirs, Steven Hite, Stacey Holman, Ellen Horne, Pamela Horton, Daniel Horwitz, Jenny Howe, Lee-Sean Huang, Tasneem Husain, Alexandra Hynes, Roy Ip, Reena Isaac, Karen G. Jackson, Tim Jensen, Beverly Jernigan, Josean Jimenez, Alexis Johnson, Ali Jouzdani, Eirini Kaissaratou, Jeff Kaplan, Laurence A. Kaplan, Jake Katz, Michael G. Katz, Anat Kaufman, Alexandra Kaufmann, Sarah Kelly, Emily Kelsch, Samantha Kennedy, Nina Kiernan, David Kim, Allison Kirby, Lauren Klein, Sarah K. Kozlowski, Alison Kriviskey, Bruce M. Kriviskey, Tim Kutach, Dea Larson, Nichole Byrne Lau, Samantha Lazarus, Eugene Lee, Risha Lee, Jennifer A. Lee, Kari Leeper, Amelia Lester, Michael Levi, Duncan Levin, Steve Levine, Benjamin Lima, Kristin Lindner, Jes Logan, Matthew Lombardi, Stephen G. Long, Ayanna Lonian, Natalie Louie, Josh Loving, Ginger Lowry, Jennifer Luddy, Kerry Lusignan, Jane Baxter Lynn, Zachary Mallavia, Will Manlove, Edward T. Mannix, III, Paul A. Mardas, Olga Gonzalez Marruffo, Andrea Marsh, Jonathan Martel, Moira Bessette Martin, Thomas Martin, Dan Martinez, Beth Martinez, Tom McCasland, Lindsey McCormack, Sally McDaniel, Caroline McLean, Megan McMahon, Walter J. McMahon, Erin McReynolds, Michael Macedo Meazell, Elsa Mehary, Ferne Mele, David Menschel, Elizabeth Merrill, Christiane Metral, Charles H. Michelet, George I. Miller, Jaclyn Miller, Samantha Miller, Julie Mischlich, Tejal Mody, Dorothy Molnar, Amy E. Moran, Chris Mrema, Matthias Mueller, Clare Kogire Murumba, Luke Murumba, Keren Murumba, Matthew Murumba, Samuel Murumba, Vinay B. Nair, Joe Napolitano, Stew Navarre, Daniel Nelson, Monika Powe Nelson, Catherine New, Martin A.

Experimental blind tasters *continued*

Nowak, Justin Nowell, Thomas Nowell, Louis Orenstein, Anne Ouimette, Debbie Padon, Tom Pappalardo, William Parra, Lisa Parrish, Akshay Patil, Drew Patterson, Elizabeth Morrison Petegorsky, Stephen Petegorsky, Isaure de Pontbriand, Charles B. Powers, Ron Prashker, Jennie Pries, Risher Randall, Andrea Ranft, Greg Ranft, Ofir Reichenberg, Taj Reid, Julee Resendez, George Reynolds, Elizabeth Richmond-Garza, Matt Rigney, Bob A. Rivollier, Gerrit Rogers, Medora M. Rogers, Patrick Rohan, Kayla Rosenberg, Benjamin Rosenblum, Daniel Rosenblum, Murry Rosenblum, Debbie Rosmarin, Jori Ross, Elizabeth A. Rovere, Mary Pat Roy, Michael J. Roy, Denise Ruhl, James Saccento, Kate Drake Saccento, Jane Sackett, M. Melinda Sanders, Sherri Sandifer, Susan Sandikcioglu, Jorge Sanhueza-Lyon, Ruben Sanz Ramiro, Sue Schmidt, Tatiana Schnur, Peter Schultz, Joseph A. Sena, Jr., Taylor Senatore, Rachel Shiffrin, Erin Sibley, Jeff Siegel, Leslie Silbert, Will Silverman, Mark Simmelkjaes, Emily Singer, Alison D. Smith, Sarah Smith, Michael Sobolevsky, John P. Sobolweski, Claude A. Solliard, Linda K. Sparks, Joel Spiro, Ashley St. Clair, Chanel Eve Stark, Kelly Stecker, Judith Stinson, Robert C. Stinson, Brian Stubbs, Sue Stubbs, Kari Sullivan, Marty Sullivan, Linda Summers, Sara Jane Summers, Adam Taplin, Laura Tatum, Cody Taylor, Mary Taylor, Andrew Teich, Antonia Thomas, Elana Thurston-Milgrom, Melissa Tischler, Eric Titner, Anne Todd, Bruce Tolda, Darya Trapeznikova, Cynthia Urrutia, Justin Vann, Holly M. Veech, Alan Verson, Matt Verson, Paula Verson, A. Vora, Preeya Vyas, Johannes Walker, Brad Wall, Ruth Waser, Jillian Wein, Thomas Weiner, Andrew Whitcomb, Kirk Wickline, Cynthia M. Williams, Lisa Michelle Wilmore, Elsie E. Wilmoth, Rae Wilson, Clarence Wine, Matt Wong, Betty Yip, Randy Yost, Richard Young, Justin Yu, George R. Zimmerman, Donald H. Zuckerman, Donna E. Zuckerman, Monwabisi Zukani

Contents

Fearless Critic
restaurant guides

Brutally honest reviews. By undercover chefs and food nerds.
No restaurant ads. In print and online at **fearlesscritic.com**.

fearlesscritic.com

Preface to the new 2010 edition

For millennia, our civilizations have understood that beauty can come from fermentation, unexpected happiness from unintended rot. For wine drinkers, the global economic rot of recent years has yielded at least one happy byproduct: a decline in the prices of premium wines, more interest in value wines, and a much-improved lineup of bottles under $15.

We see this not as a wave of panicked price-slashing on the part of producers, importers, and distributors, but rather as a natural correction in an overpriced market. That correction is good news for all of us, because it has encouraged everyone along the wine chain—from producers to retailers to sommeliers—to focus more of their attention on delicious wines that are also affordable, and less of it on the so-called "lifestyle marketing" that, for decades, has propped up the prices of prestige wines.

This has also resulted in some long-overdue airtime from major media outlets for the everyday wines that most Americans are actually drinking. Blind tasting has risen onto the radar screen of the everyday wine drinker—and even onto Hollywood's, with a big-budget film about Steven Spurrier's famous 1976 blind tasting of California wines against French wines, the "Judgment of Paris."

Yet amidst all of this, there is still a haze that surrounds the experience of buying wine. Arbitrary pricing is still the norm. Wine critics' 100-point ratings seem to make less sense than ever. And consolidated wine companies, operating from the bottom end to the top end, continue to upend wine's traditional labeling hierarchy with graphically aggressive wine packaging that seems designed to shock, or at least to make you giggle.

An incipient industry of international negociants has even begun to label wines in a way that renders their countries of origin opaque. Over time, amateur wine enthusiasts learn to anticipate what a red Burgundy or a New Zealand Sauvignon Blanc is going to taste like, but how is *anyone* supposed to know what to expect from a wine called "Smoking Loon," "Fat Bastard," or "Bitch"?

Even as prices fall and inexpensive wines garner more attention, the wines most widely available in America—from Yellow Tail to Veuve Clicquot—are being marketed with a method once reserved for fashion and cosmetics: by selling an image, a lifestyle, a place in the social world.

Yet our blind tastings have shown, again and again, that people consistently prefer a $9 Spanish Cava to that $40 Veuve—and even to a $150 Dom Pérignon. In fact, when we served 6,000 glasses of wine hidden in brown paper bags to more than 500 people—a large-scale experiment on a diverse mix of wine experts and everyday wine drinkers—we found that, on the whole, people actually preferred the cheaper wines to the more expensive wines.

The haze over the wine world is thicker than ever, and it is our goal to help our readers see through it.

Part I of this book—the "blind tasting manifesto"—discusses these results in light of some of the most cutting-edge work in behavioral economics and neuroscience. Whether or not you're a wine expert, we aim to challenge some of your most basic assumptions about wine, and to encourage you to question the orthodoxy that governs wine pricing and wine rating.

Part II—the 2010 Wine Trials themselves—aims to help you better navigate the inexpensive wine shelf. *The Wine Trials 2010* reveals and reviews 150 winning wines under $15 that outscored $50 to $150 bottles in a series of rigorous brown-bag blind tasting competitions conducted by our editors this year.

Aside from reviewing an entirely new lineup of wines and expanding the number of bottles reviewed to 150 from 100, we have made some other important changes since our last edition. First, we have lowered our production minimum for inclusion to 20,000 cases from 50,000.[1] This has allowed us to include some interesting wines that are widely available around the country but aren't quite as mass-produced as some of their counterparts.

Second, we have introduced a new nomination system for the selection of wines to be tasted. We have accepted nominations from professionals in many different areas of the wine industry, from producers to sommeliers, importers to retailers, creating an initial selection of the 450 widely available wines under $15 that people within the industry like best.

The second phase—the blind tastings themselves—narrowed the pool again by more than two-thirds, to the 150 *Wine Trials* winners presented in Part II. Each of these wines outscored much more expensive bottles in our brown-bag blind tastings. We think the result is a rich, diverse, carefully chosen pool of wines that will bring you some of the best pleasure-to-dollar ratios on the market.

Every wine in the book is recommended as one of the best widely available values under $15, beating out hundreds of other carefully chosen wines that did *not* meet the bar. We have not rated wines numerically in this book; we believe wine tasting to be too subjective and nebulous to be boiled down to a single number.

We did, however, want to bestow awards upon the wines that did the very best in our tastings. As such, we chose a set of finalists—the wines our editors liked best in the first round of blind tastings—and we held a playoff blind tasting in which we selected a winner in each of our style categories. For the first time, we have also chosen one *Wine Trials* Wine of the Year and one *Wine Trials* Winery of the Year.

None of the tasting results from our last edition were counted for this edition; every wine tasted in the 2010 trials has been newly released since the first edition. The 48 repeat winners in *The Wine Trials 2010* each represent a new release or new vintage of the wine that won in the last edition. Of course, that also means that 52 of last year's winners *didn't* make this year's top 150. There is a commonly held belief that inexpensive, higher-production wines don't tend to change much from year to year. This is a myth. Although more expensive, smaller-production wines are generally *more* sensitive to the vagaries of weather, it's not at all true that inexpensive wines don't vary with the vintage.

These variations often have as much to do with changes in winemaking *style* as they have to do with differences in the climate. This year, for instance, our blind tasters noticed sparkling wines with more added sugar and California Chardonnays with less oak. Such phenomena, along with the thousands of new bottles put onto the market every year, make it absolutely crucial for us to release a new edition of *The Wine Trials* annually.

Although Part II may be more useful as a buyer's guide, we do hope you take the time to read Part I as well. This year's blind tasting manifesto is completely revised and updated, and discusses a good deal of new scientific research that has come out since the first edition. We also dive into some of the lively debate that this book's first edition set off in the print media and blogosphere.

Our hope is that once you're armed with gustatory information instead of marketing *mis*information, you will be better able to choose wines whose regions and styles correspond to what you actually like. Once you start blind tasting, you will be better able to develop a set of preferences that's uniquely yours, not guided by prices, magazine critics, or brands. That's not to say that you, too—if you're not already an expert—won't come to like expensive wine more as your knowledge of wine grows.

But don't be too surprised if your preferences, even as they become more sophisticated, never turn out to match up well to the hierarchical structure that currently dominates the industry. The most important point of all is to take our thoughts and recommendations as starting points, not endpoints; to blind taste yourself; and to write to the authors at fearless@fearlesscritic.com if you would like to comment on anything we have to say.

This book is dedicated to the idea that blind tasting can help us stop spending too much money on wines we *don't* really like, and that it can help us start spending less money on wines we really *do* like. There are a lot of social, psychological, and informational obstacles blocking the way to that goal. Within these pages, we will provide you with a map around those obstacles, a guide to developing trust in your own palate, and a short treatise on the ways that the modern market fails us when we outsource our taste to others. We hope that you find it helpful.

–Robin Goldstein and Alexis Herschkowitsch

Part I The blind tasting manifesto
by Robin Goldstein

Chapter 1 Blind taste

Dom Pérignon, a $150 Champagne from France, and Domaine Ste. Michelle Cuvée Brut, a $12 sparkling wine from Washington State, are both made in the traditional Champagne method. Both wines are widely available at wine stores, liquor stores, and restaurants. Both are dry, with high acidity. The two bottles are more or less the same size and shape. So why are consumers willing to pay more than 12 times more for one than for the other?

The most obvious explanation would be that, to most wine drinkers, the liquid inside the bottle of Dom Pérignon tastes better than the liquid inside the bottle of Domaine Ste. Michelle—if not 12 times better, then at least somewhat better.[2] However, that doesn't seem to be the case. Between fall 2007 and spring 2008, we conducted an experiment serving these two sparkling wines head-to-head in five different blind tastings, with the bottles hidden inside brown paper bags. And 41 of 62 tasters—about two thirds—preferred the Domaine Ste. Michelle.

In October 2009, we replicated the experiment on a smaller scale with newer releases of the two sparkling wines. This time, we served them to a group of professional chefs, certified sommeliers, and food writers, of which more than 70% preferred the humble $12 bottle to the famous $150 one. This time, we also threw in Veuve Clicquot, a popular $40 Champagne from the same luxury products group—LVMH—that makes Dom Pérignon. More than 85% of tasters preferred the Domaine Ste. Michelle to the Veuve.

This doesn't seem to be a single, idiosyncratic instance in which people's tastes happen to run contrary to popular wisdom or market prices. The Champagne battle described above was just a small part of a series of blind tastings that we conducted around the country over that same time span. It was an experiment in which we poured more than 6,000 glasses of wine from brown-bagged bottles that cost from $1.50 to $150.

The result? As a whole, the group actually preferred the cheaper wines to the more expensive wines—by a statistically significant margin.

The 507 blind tasters in this 2007–2008 experiment represented many different segments of the wine-buying world. They were professionals in a wide range of fields. Some were wine experts, others everyday wine drinkers. They included New York City sommeliers and Harvard professors, winemakers from France, neuroscientists and artists, top chefs and college students, doctors and lawyers, wine importers and wine store owners, novelists and economists, TV comedy writers and oenologists, bartenders and grad students, 21-year-olds and 88-year-olds, socialists and conservatives, heavy drinkers and lightweights.

On the whole, tasters preferred a (then-)nine-dollar Beringer Founders' Estate Cabernet Sauvignon to a $120 wine from the same grape and the same producer: Beringer Private Reserve Cabernet Sauvignon. They preferred a six-dollar Vinho Verde from Portugal to a $40 Cakebread Chardonnay and a $50 Chassagne-Montrachet 1er Cru from Louis Latour. And when we concealed the labels and prices of 27 sparkling wines and asked people to rate them, the Dom Pérignon finished 17th—behind 14 sparkling wines that cost less than $15, eight of which cost less than $10.[3]

Does this mean that the $12 Domaine Ste. Michelle is *objectively better* than the $150 bottle of Dom? In an abstract, Platonic sense—or by established industry norms—perhaps not. In fact, the wine experts among our tasters didn't dislike the expensive wines in the way that everyday wine drinkers did; they liked more expensive wines as much, or even a bit more, than cheaper wines.

But the vast majority of wine consumers are everyday wine drinkers, not experts. At a minimum, it seems clear that many Americans might be wasting at least $138, at least where taste is concerned, when they buy Dom Pérignon for special occasions.

There is a mounting body of evidence from within and without the wine world that wine pricing is more arbitrary than one might assume, but ours was one of the first studies to show an *inverse* correlation between price and preference. That inverse correlation was moderate but statistically significant across all of our tasters ($p=0.038$; this means that there was only a 3.8% probability that our results came about by chance—in the sciences, the generally accepted standard for statistical significance is a p value of less than 0.05). When you exclude the very cheapest and most expensive wines and just look at the mid-range wines—those priced between $6 and $15—the effect is even stronger ($p=0.004$).

We did not allow the tasters to discuss the wines with each other before rating them, and we kept the wines concealed in their numbered brown paper bags until after the evaluation forms had been turned in. In order to weigh the results of consistent tasters more than inconsistent tasters, we subjected people to the "twin-wine test," serving them two identical wines in the same flight of six—unbeknownst to the tasters, of course. With the help of our statistics team, we gave less weight to the opinions of tasters who rated the identical wines differently.

The results of our experiment are explained in technical form in the appendix, written by economists Johan Almenberg and Anna Dreber Almenberg, and they are also presented in an academic paper that we published in the *Journal of Wine Economics* entitled "Do More Expensive Wines Taste Better?".[4]

By no means are all wine critics and commentators in denial of this effect. Many have commented on the arbitrariness of pricing, including Master of Wine Jancis Robinson, one of the world's foremost wine writers, who has observed a "lack of correlation between price and pleasure." She writes: "Perhaps it is not so surprising that a first-rate example of a little-known wine can seem much more memorable than something more famous selling at ten times the price...What is more extraordinary is the wild price variation at the very top end. Demand bubbles up mysteriously, apparently fuelled by fashion and rumour as much as by intrinsic quality."[5]

In their seminal 1976 book on wine quality measurement, *Wines: Their Sensory Evaluation*, UC Davis professors Maynard Amerine (an oenologist) and Edward Roessler (a mathematician) tend to concur, although they, like Robinson, focus on the overpricing of super-premium wines: "[P]rice depends on many factors that are not necessarily related to quality. Those who buy wines on a price basis deserve what they get. ... Some famous vineyards, secure in the knowledge that they have an established market, often charge whatever the market will bear."[6]

Between 1997 and 2001, researchers Sébastien Lecocq and Michael Visser conducted three large-scale expert blind tastings of a total of 1,409 wines from Bordeaux and Burgundy under highly controlled conditions with professional tasters from the Institut National de la Consommation. They found that the tasters' sensory evaluations of the wines were only very weakly correlated with price, leading Lecocq and Visser to conclude that "the market price of Bordeaux wine can be explained primarily by the objective characteristics appearing on the label of the bottle." Those tastings involved only experts, but Lecocq and Visser foreshadow our results with everyday wine drinkers when they suggest that "when non-experts blind-taste cheap and expensive wines they typically tend to prefer the cheaper ones."[7]

In a series of blind tastings conducted by Hilke Plassmann, Antonio Rangel, and their colleagues at Stanford Business School and Cal Tech—part of an important brain-scanning study that I'll come back to in chapter 2—everyday wine drinkers rated the cheap wines *higher* than they rated the expensive wines, just as they did in our blind tastings. And in an experiment conducted by Roman Weil, which will be discussed in chapter 3, everyday wine drinkers didn't prefer reserve wines to regular wines, even though the wines differed in price by an order of magnitude. Our observations, like those of the scholars above, could hardly contrast any more starkly with the patterns of wine ratings on the 100-point scales used by magazine critics, which tend to track wine prices consistently (see chapter 3 for evidence of that).

What is going on here? If blind tasting experiments show that wine pricing is arbitrary from the perspective of everyday wine drinkers, then why are the magazine ratings that those drinkers rely on so directly correlated with price? And why do everyday wine drinkers still trust those ratings, and spend money on expensive wine?

Chapter 2 The taste of money

Moët & Chandon, the producer of Dom Pérignon, sells more than 60 million bottles of premium-priced Champagne every year—most of them to everyday wine drinkers, not wine professionals. Putting aside our results for a moment, it's hard to imagine that millions of consumers would be buying $30 to $150 Champagnes and really, truly enjoying them less than $10 sparkling wines. Most of those people must *feel*, at least, that they're getting their money's worth; otherwise, presumably, they wouldn't keep buying expensive Champagne.[8]

The sheer number of amateur wine bloggers on the Internet at the moment, many of whom spend hours every day writing extensive reviews for no pay, seems evidence enough to demonstrate wine lovers' passionate enjoyment of expensive wine. It would seem ludicrous to suggest that amateur wine lovers are not really enjoying their $2,000 bottles of Château Margaux or Screaming Eagle, or to suspect their passion to be anything less than genuine. Yet even that passion seems to conflict with our results—and with the results of scientists in wine economics and cognition.

What do we make, for instance, of the work of wine researcher Frédéric Brochet, who fooled 57 French wine experts by serving them two identical wines, one in an expensive Grand Cru bottle, the other in a cheap Vin de Table bottle? Although both bottles contained the same wine—a mid-range Bordeaux—Brochet's subjects preferred the wine from the Grand Cru bottle by a dramatic margin. They used positive terms like "excellent," "good," "complex," and "long" more than twice as often when describing the supposed Grand Cru as they did when describing the supposed Vin de Table, and, conversely, used negative terms like "unbalanced," "short," "flat," and "simple" more than twice as much when describing the supposed Vin de Table.

Another of Brochet's experiments showed that, like price, the color of a wine can affect subjects' reported experiences. When 54 subjects tasted a white wine under normal conditions, they tended to use typical white-wine descriptors (e.g. "fresh," "lemon," "apricot," and "honey") to describe their experience. But when they tasted that same white wine colored with a flavorless dye to look like red wine, the tasters switched to typical red-wine descriptors (e.g. "red currant," "cherry," "raspberry," and "spice"). The influence of the wine's color on their taste experience, or at least their judgment, was profound.[9]

A couple of decades earlier, in *Wines: Their Sensory Evaluation*, Amerine and Roessler anticipate Brochet's results: "It is surprising," they write, "how many so-called wine experts are 'label drinkers.' Their sensory judgment is based on the source or reputation of the wine, or its producer, or the year of production."

But what do they mean by "sensory judgment"? Is it wine drinkers' *judgment* of the experience that's altered by the knowledge that a wine is expensive, or is it the *experience itself*?

I believe it to be the latter: it's the experience itself that changes once you know the wine is expensive. I do not believe that most wine drinkers simply pretend to like wine better because it's expensive, and I do not believe that they are lying to others, or even to themselves, when they report getting more pleasure from premium-priced wine.

I believe that wine actually tastes better when you know it's expensive, in every meaningful sense of the word "taste." For wine as for medicine, the placebo effect is not a mere delusion; it is a physical reality. The experience of sipping a wine you know to be expensive, then, is a real taste experience. It is the taste of money.

The best evidence that the placebo effect can change the experience of drinking itself comes from an article co-authored by a member of our Scientific Advisory Board, Shane Frederick of MIT's Sloan School of Management, along with his MIT colleague Dan Ariely, author of the new book *Predictably Irrational*, and Leonard Lee of Columbia Business School. It's a study about beer.

In 1964, it had been shown that beer drinkers, under experimental conditions, didn't prefer their favorite beers in blind tastings when the labels were hidden.[10] Several decades later, Frederick and Ariely, who were interested in pinning down the precise moment at which sensory experience was shaped and preferences formed, ran a complex experiment that involved adding balsamic vinegar to beer before serving it.

Here's how it worked: 388 tasters were randomly assigned to three different groups. The first group of tasters rated both beers—with and without vinegar—with no information about the ingredients, and 59% of them preferred the beer with vinegar (apparently, for many people, balsamic vinegar can improve the taste of beer). Tasters in the second group were instead informed of the ingredients before tasting; of that group, only 30% preferred the beer with vinegar. Their negative expectations seem to have colored their experience and reduced the pleasure they got from drinking the vinegared beer. Most interesting, however, were the tasters in the third group, who were told about the vinegar *after* tasting it, but *before* rating it. That group, like the first group, preferred the vinegared beer—even though they knew it contained vinegar before assigning their ratings. The first and third groups did not differ significantly in their preferences.[11]

The punch line is that the knowledge that there was vinegar in the beer affected people's *taste experience* if they were told about it beforehand, but it didn't significantly change their *judgment* of the beer after they'd already tasted it. To me, this is strong evidence that expectations exert more influence on the level of taste *experience* than they do on the level of taste *judgment*.

In 2009, Johan Almenberg and Anna Dreber Almenberg carried out an interesting variation on Frederick and Ariely's experiment with wine, varying the moment at which the price of a cheap ($5) or expensive ($40) wine was revealed. Interestingly, they found a more powerful priming effect in women than in men.[12] This possible gender difference certainly merits further exploration.

One of the most talked-about wine articles in years has come from Hilke Plassmann, Antonio Rangel, and their colleagues at

Stanford Business School and the California Institute of Technology, who added a set of fMRI brain-scan results to this remarkable body of evidence.[13] fMRI—short for functional magnetic resonance imaging—is a brain-scanning technology that (roughly speaking) measures changes in blood flow to different parts of the brain over time. There are some major drawbacks to the technique; for instance, subjects must lie very still inside a cylinder, which is obviously a bit different from the way we normally enjoy wine. More importantly, subjects in fMRI experiments have to sip liquids from a tube—so they don't get to swirl and smell the wine.

Still, Plassmann and Rangel's results are fascinating. In their experiment, 20 subjects in fMRI machines were told that they would taste five different Cabernet Sauvignon wines whose retail prices were $5, $10, $35, $45, and $90. In reality, the subjects were only served three wines: a $5 wine, a $45 wine, and a $90 wine. They were served the $5 wine twice, once while being told it cost $45 and once while being told its real cost. Likewise, they were served the $90 wine twice, once while being told it cost $10.

If you've read up to this point in the book, you probably won't be surprised by what happened: subjects' preferences correlated with the *fake* prices of the wines, not with the *actual* prices. When people thought they were drinking $90 wine, they loved it, even if it was actually $10 wine. What's more, blood flow to a brain area commonly associated with pleasure—the left medial orbitofrontal cortex—also was correlated with the fake price of the wines, but not with the actual price. For the first time, the neural correlates of price expectations *creating* pleasure were visible.

In a footnote to their study, Plassmann and Rangel had their subjects taste the same wines a few weeks later during a "post-experimental session without price cues"—that is, a straight-up blind tasting. And in that tasting, subjects actually preferred the $5 wine to the $90 wine. Sound familiar?

The wine placebo effect is real. We must accept that truth about ourselves. It doesn't mean that wine aficionados and experts are con artists, nor does it mean that people don't legitimately sense pleasurable qualities in very expensive wine, even when they taste it blind. But it does mean that when we don't taste blind, it's almost impossible to know whether the pleasure of expensive wine is coming from its own taste, or from the taste of money.

Chapter 3 The perfect palate?

From 2000 to 2007, *Wine Spectator* rated 6,475 wines that cost $10 or less. Of those, only three of them—four hundredths of one percent—scored above 90 on the magazine's 100-point scale, and none scored above 91. By comparison, for those same vintages, of the 2,490 wines reviewed in *Wine Spectator* that cost $100 or more, 1,781 of them—more than 71%—scored above 90. *Wine Enthusiast* tells a similar story: of the 5,896 wines from the 2000 to 2007 vintages listed at $10 or less in their database, only two scored above 91.[14]

Could these numbers really reflect the tasters' experiences? Taste and smell, the so-called "chemical senses," are the most fickle and least quantifiable of our sensory systems. When people rate tastes and smells, the variance in their results tends to be extraordinarily high, even in the most controlled of cognitive tests. And wine is one of the most volatile organic substances that we ingest.

Considering wine's high sensitivity to oxygen, to temperature, and to time—complicated further by the physical unpredictability of our palates—the degree of correlation between price and qualitative score in the mainstream wine publications has become harder and harder to accept with each additional scientific study published on the subject. How could our results diverge so dramatically from the magazine critics' opinions?

Let's put aside, for a moment, the implausibility of the notion that *Wine Spectator*'s price-score correlation could have occurred naturally under controlled blind tasting conditions with *any* tasters. The most obvious explanation for this disconnect would then be that expensive wine is simply an acquired taste, and that the vast majority of wine drinkers—like the subjects of the experiments cited above, including ours—just haven't acquired that taste the way that these elite tasters have. Perhaps the magazines have cornered the market on critics who have "perfect palates"—the rare ability to taste something totally different in these expensive wines, something that simply *could not exist* in a $10 bottle. Maybe it's something that amateur wine drinkers, and even many wine experts, just can't detect, or—alternatively—can detect, but dislike.

Roman Weil, a professor of accounting at the University of Chicago, has shown that non-experts' preferences seem to have little do to with experts' ratings. In a fascinating study, he served blind tastes of the same wine from two different vintages, one that had been deemed "good" by wine experts, the other deemed "bad." Tasters also compared a prestigious reserve bottling against a regular bottling, again blind. In both cases, the tasters didn't do much better than chance at telling the two wines apart, and even when they did, they were as likely to prefer the cheap bottle as the expensive bottle—even though, in both cases, the prices differed by an order of magnitude. So for Weil's everyday wine drinkers, choosing the wines lauded by the critics didn't translate to any additional pleasure—when they tasted blind, of course.[15]

Weil did not administer his test to wine experts, but there is evidence that experts and everyday wine drinkers do have different taste in wine. Within the subset of wine experts in our blind tastings, there was a slight *positive* correlation—rather than a negative one—between price and preference. Still, the effect was only marginally significant, and our experts' opinions were nowhere near as price-correlated as are those of the *Wine Spectator* critics'. Neither were the opinions of Lecocq and Visser's wine experts. In fact, to my knowledge, no scientific blind-tasting study of wine experts has ever shown expensive wines to do as consistently well, or cheap wines to do as consistently poorly, as they do in *Wine Spectator*.

There is one particularly compelling recent piece of evidence that wine experts' results, like the results from non-experts, might be characterized more by inconsistency than by consistency. It comes from Robert Hodgson, a retired oceanography and statistics professor who also runs a small winery called Fieldbrook in Humboldt County, a region better known for other crops.

For years, like other small winemakers looking for ways to distinguish their wines from the competition, Hodgson would submit his wines to various medal competitions in California and elsewhere. But the results seemed to have no pattern at all. At one competition, one wine would win a gold medal, while another would win no medal at all; at another competition, the results were precisely reversed.

The judges at these competitions were experts in the field—winemakers, oenologists, wine writers, and such. Yet the more competitions Hodgson entered, the more suspicious he became that the results were coming out more or less random, and that the best way to win medals was not to make the best wine possible, but rather to simply enter as many competitions as possible.

Testing that hypothesis, though, proved to be a difficult task. The problem was that while information about which wines *won* medals is readily accessible, information about which wines entered but *didn't* win is much harder to come by. After a lot of searching, Hodgson finally found what he was looking for in a complex data set of more than 4,000 entries into 13 U.S. wine competitions in 2003.

Hodgson's analysis, published in the *Journal of Wine Economics* in spring 2009, investigated the degree of consistency between expert judges' blind-tasting ratings of the same wines in different competitions. His evidence indicated that "[there is] almost no consensus among the 13 wine competitions regarding wine quality"; that "for wines receiving a gold medal in one or more competitions, it is very likely that the same wine received no award at another"; and that "the likelihood of receiving a gold medal can be statistically explained by chance alone."

Although some of Hodgson's more radical conclusions have been debated, what seems clear from his work, at least, is this: when anyone—even a top wine expert—assigns a numerical rating to wine, even if there is some signal, there is definitely a whole lot of noise. But where is the noise in those *Wine Spectator* results? Are their critics superhuman? Are they really tasting blind?

Before I go any further, let me be clear that the points I'm making in this chapter refer largely to wine magazines: *Wine Spectator,* Robert Parker's *Wine Advocate*, *Wine Enthusiast*, and so on. There are numerous great wine critics and writers out there—many of whom write for newspapers, or who maintain wine blogs—to whom this critique does not apply. Some critics *do* taste blind, and many don't use numerical ratings for wines. However, in the modern wine industry, Robert Parker and *Wine Spectator*—perhaps in part because of the mere fact that they *do* assign 100-point ratings—exert a more powerful influence over the industry, and over price trends, than do the other critics.

So, do the magazine critics taste blind? Well, Robert Parker himself, for one—the father of the US wine-magazine industry and inventor of the 100-point rating scale—doesn't. He freely admits that he sometimes rates wine based on non-blind tasting. This is just one of the axes on which his integrity has been increasingly questioned lately. Wine blogger Tyler Colman, who goes by "Dr. Vino," has undertaken a fascinating series of exposés of Parker and his staff, first (in April 2009) reporting that Parker's right-hand man at the *Wine Advocate,* Jay Miller, had accepted lavish junkets—private plane rides and such—from various coalitions of foreign wine producers.[16]

A couple of years ago, I became similarly curious about the integrity of *Wine Spectator*, whose high scores correlate with high prices just as Parker's do. I undertook an investigation of the magazine's restaurant awards program, the "Wine Spectator Awards of Excellence," which supposedly honors the restaurants with the best wine programs in the world. The magazine also charges restaurants a $250 "entry fee" to participate. I was curious about whether the Awards of Excellence program, which grosses well over $1 million annually for the magazine, represented real expert judgment, or whether it really just functioned as an advertising scheme.

To find out, I decided to apply for an award myself. I created a fictitious Milan restaurant, "Osteria L'Intrepido," whose high-priced "reserve wine list" was composed almost entirely of *Wine*

Spectator's lowest-rated Italian wines from the past couple of decades. These were the wines with ratings in the 60s and 70s— wines deemed undrinkable by *Wine Spectator*'s own critics. And I priced them in the hundreds of euros.

I posted that wine list on a website I created for the imaginary restaurant. I submitted an application for Osteria L'Intrepido along with the $250 fee, jumped through all the requisite hoops, and lo and behold, I won the Award of Excellence, as published in the August 2008 issue of *Wine Spectator*. The only communication I ever received from *Wine Spectator*, at any point, was one voicemail informing me that I'd won the award, and asking if I'd like to purchase an additional $3,000 to $8,000 in advertising in the issue to further publicize my award. The story and materials are still up on my blog at blindtaste.com.[17]

So what happened after the "Awards of Excellence" program was revealed to be a massive million-dollar fraud, an abuse of expert authority, a violation of the public trust for pure financial gain? Not even so much as an apology to their own readers.

Interestingly, though, the magazine still makes almost as big a deal about blind wine tasting as I do. James Laube, one of *Wine Spectator*'s senior editors, has gone so far as to write a blog entry about the importance of blind tasting. "*Wine Spectator* has always believed in blind tastings," Laube explains. "We know the region, the vintage and the grape variety, if relevant. But we don't know the producer or the price."[18]

Consider that statement for a moment: the magazine critics are tasting blind, but they know the region, the vintage, and the grape variety. Let's say it's a red wine, the appellation is Hermitage,[19] and the vintage is 2005. The cheapest possible wine in the *Wine Spectator* database that would fit those criteria costs $49. And, to their credit, these tasters certainly know enough about wine to know that Hermitage reds are going to be expensive. In that example, then, they *would* know the price, or at least the price category, before tasting—which means that they wouldn't really be tasting blind. They'd know that they were tasting expensive wines, and they'd have full frontal exposure to the placebo effect.

At least Laube admits that his staff is only human. "Even the professionals 'miss' a wine now and then," writes Laube, "the same way the refs miss a call. But we believe that if we can eliminate any possibility of bias, we're at least giving you a fair and honest assessment of the wines." Luckily for Laube, it seems that his team of professionals hasn't "missed a call" and accidentally scored a wine under $10 above 91 in at least the past 6,475 tries.

One of the more compelling scenes in the 2004 documentary film *Mondovino* depicts fashion-empire heir and wine producer Salvatore Ferragamo hanging out with James Suckling, the *Wine Spectator* critic who rates Ferragamo's wine for the magazine. If you haven't seen *Mondovino*, it's worth it just to check out this priceless little scene, which could be straight out of *Borat*: the joke's on Suckling, but he doesn't seem to know it.

Suckling seems to fancy himself a sort of ambassador for Italian wine in the modern era: "Italian wine is the wine of our generation," says Suckling. "Our parents drank French wines, wore Hèrmes, went to Paris. Our generation, we wear Armani, Ferragamo...Prada, and then we drink Italian wines, eat Italian food, and travel to Florence, Rome, Venice." Talking about the 90 he's awarded to Ferragamo's wine, Suckling says: "I was generous, I thought. But he is my landlord." Then the two joke about the idea of renegotiating Suckling's rent for a 95.

None of the evidence in *Mondovino*—or anywhere else—is quite sufficient to prove that there's any actual corruption going on. Suckling and Ferragamo, of course, are just joking around when they talk about paying for high ratings. And it's not quite *impossible*—just statistically improbable—that *Wine Spectator* critics are among the only people in the world with perfect palates.

But what kind of message does it send that the magazine continues to accept and publish full-page advertisements for many of the same wines it's reviewing and scoring? And what kind of message does it send to everyday wine drinkers that Suckling—and, by extension, *Wine Spectator*—openly flaunts a buddy-buddy relationship with the producer whose wines he's scoring?

It is particularly fitting, I think, that Suckling should be hanging out with a fashion maven, of all people. Because, as I suggest in the next chapter, the wine industry and its magazine critics (not to mention its judges of "excellence" in restaurant wine programs) are looking more like fashionistas every day.

And in the end, corrupt or not corrupt, placebo effects or perfect palates, the problem is the same: magazine critics' results have little in common with the palates of everyday wine drinkers. Why, then, would everyday wine drinkers expect that they'd be any more likely to enjoy a 95-point wine than an 80-point wine? Why, for that matter, should everyday wine drinkers pay any attention at all to those numerical ratings?

Chapter 4 Dom Pérignon's new clothes

So far we've seen that human beings are pretty suggestible when it comes to wine. The suggestion from some magazine critics, their integrity notwithstanding, is that we should like expensive wine more than cheap wine. We have also seen that when we know a wine is expensive or highly rated, we actually *do* like it more—our brains' pleasure areas even light up on brain scans. The high prices of prestigious wines have started the engine of the placebo effect, and the magazine critics' endorsement of the price-quality relationship has added fuel. But even if we like it more, there is another component that goes into our choice to spend *so much* more for expensive wine: the desire to be seen owning and drinking it.

The act of buying, serving, and drinking expensive wine, beyond the mere sensory experience, can provide a way for people to display their wealth, taste, and sophistication to other people—a form of conspicuous consumption. I think of it as an *aspirational* act: behavior driven by the aspiration to be part of the next higher social class, a token of a more expensive and desirable way of life. As such, conspicuous consumption is actually more associated with the new-money middle class than with the old-money upper class; members of the upper class tend to be less brand-driven, or at least more discreet, with their spending. That's why you see more Champagne consumed in Vegas than in Reims, where it's made.

Of course, extreme conspicuous consumption is the exception to the rule; by no means is every oenophile an aspirational consumer. But we all might have a bit more conspicuous consumption in us than we think. We're in denial, in part because when the placebo effect works, *it actually makes the wine taste good*, thus making its purchase feel more like a justified exchange at fair market value than an act of conspicuous consumption. Even if you've really paid more for the bottle, label, and marketing than you've paid for the liquid within, it rarely *feels* that way. And that's how some producers are able to get away with selling premium wines at a markup that would seem insane from any production perspective.

Nowhere is that markup more insane than in the world of sparkling wines. This might happen in part because sparkling wines are probably the most difficult of all wine categories to blind taste and compare; carbon dioxide does a pretty good job of obscuring the differences between them. When you taste sparkling wines, it's a lot easier to detect differences on the nose than on the mouth; once the bubbles hit your tongue, your ability to sense much beyond sweetness or dryness is significantly stunted.

Try this experiment: taste a couple of sparkling wines just after opening them, and jot down your notes. Then, leave the wines out and open until their fizz disappears. When you taste them again, not only will the wines have changed, they'll also seem much more different from each other than they did initially. Their acidity and oakiness, if any, will become more pronounced, and you'll detect more fruit flavors on the palate.

That's a secret that the premium Champagne producers don't want to let out. Champagne carefully guards its status as a celebratory, special-occasion wine that represents the idea that no expense was spared, whether at a glamorous New Year's Eve party or a wedding. This status makes it a fertile ground for premium markups on unremarkable wines that, in other circumstances, might not be demonstrably better than much cheaper wines.

In the 2007–2008 experiment, our blind tasters sampled more than 350 glasses of 27 sparkling wines, of which eight under $15 qualified for our top 100. All eight of these, including the $8 Segura Viudas Brut and the $9 Freixenet Cordon Negro Brut, beat both the $150 Dom Pérignon and the $40 Veuve Clicquot in our tastings. And as I mentioned in chapter 1, head to head, 41 of 62 tasters—about two thirds—in the 2007–2008 tastings preferred a

$12 Domaine Ste. Michelle Brut from Washington State to the Dom; this year, on a smaller scale, 70% preferred the Ste. Michelle to the Dom, and 85% preferred the Ste. Michelle to the Veuve.

The placebo effect aside, why shouldn't Dom and Veuve—given their perennial popularity with everyday wine drinkers, not just experts—do better, at least, than *that*?

A peek at www.lvmh.com—the website of Moët Hennessy Louis Vuitton, owner of both the Dom Pérignon and Veuve Clicquot brands—offers a clue. Aside from Champagne and those famously imitated handbags, the LVMH portfolio is a roll call of the world's aspirational luxury lifestyle brands: Acqua di Parma, Belvedere and Chopin vodka, Christian Dior perfume and watches, Château d'Yquem wine, Fendi, Givenchy, Guerlain, Kenzo, Krug, Marc Jacobs, Sephora, TAG Heuer, and so on.

The company also runs the consumer branch of De Beers, the diamond empire, and—surprise, surprise—a vast network of duty-free shops at airports around the world. LVMH, which recorded 2007 revenues of $26 billion—by comparison, Google's revenues were less than half that—is probably the world's most successful practitioner of selling conspicuous consumption. In a year that saw the worldwide economy suffer, LVMH had its best year ever.

But how much is the company actually spending on *making* Champagne? Well, they don't make that exact information public, but in 2007, LVMH reported that only 35% of revenues went toward the cost of goods, while 43%—that's $11 billion—went to the cost of sales, marketing, and overhead.[20] In contrast, Constellation Brands, the monster wine conglomerate in the US mass-market wine world, reported in its 2007 annual report that, on the cost side, 58% of revenues went toward the cost of goods, while Constellation spent just 12% of revenues on the cost of sales, marketing, and overhead:[21]

Company	2007 revenues	Cost of goods	Sales, marketing, and overhead
LVMH	$26 billion	$9 billion (35% of revenues)	$11 billion (43% of revenues)
Constellation	$6.4 billion	$3.7 billion (58% of revenues)	$768 million (12% of revenues)

It's starting to look less surprising that the liquid inside Dom Pérignon might not taste so much better than the liquid inside a much cheaper bottle: we're paying our portion of glossy advertisements, corporate sponsorships, armies of top-tier MBAs in fantastic offices, parties at the world's most exclusive nightclubs, and a payroll that includes Tiger Woods, Claudia Schiffer, Catherine Deneuve, André Agassi, Steffi Graf, and Mikhail Gorbachev (who has clearly come a long way from his work leading a communist country). And they *advertise* that payroll. Why do we fall for it?

Well, flip through LVMH's 2007 annual report, and you'll discover that the company seems to have found the consumer-products-industry holy grail: a rare phenomenon known in economics as a Veblen good. Microeconomic theory predicts that the demand for a normal good decreases when the price goes up. But Veblen goods—named for the social theorist Thorstein Veblen, author of *The Theory of the Leisure Class*—are things that people actually want *more* when the price is raised.

Justin Weinberg, a philosopher at the University of South Carolina, has suggested that expensive wines often function as Veblen goods—that a wine's high price alone can be "sufficient to stimulate a strong interest in consuming it."[22] In the case of premium-priced Champagne, the more it costs, the more impressive it is—even to ourselves. In some cases, the pleasure we're getting from the expensive bottle might even have virtually nothing to do with what's inside, and everything to do with the label, the image, and simply the price we've paid.

That language might sound familiar to the authors of the LVMH annual report, who boasted that over the past year, "the [Champagne] brand continued its very strong international media presence through the 'Be Fabulous' promotional campaign. ... The Wines and Spirits business group recorded organic revenue growth of 13%, driven by the increase in volumes...and the implementation of a policy to raise prices." The report continues: "the Moët Hennessy distribution network applied the planned price increases, thus strengthening its premium positioning."

Increase the price of Champagne to *strengthen* positioning?

LVMH seems to know they've got a Veblen good on their hands, and they can barely contain the enthusiasm (within the constraints of sedate Wall Street lingo, anyway) to convey that point to their shareholders. But they also seem to know that they can only continue to pull it off if they keep marketing their wine like a perfume, a diamond ring, a leather bag, or a Swiss watch, which means keeping Woods, Schiffer, and Gorbachev on board, too, and spending billions doing it.

At some point, the annual report moves on to Cognac, un-ironically describing the "major promotional plans" that "enhanced and intensified the dynamic image of the brand," telling of "an advertising campaign...titled Flaunt Your Taste," which "gave Hennessy high visibility and an enhanced image of sophistication."

"Flaunt Your Taste." Veblen couldn't have put it any better had he worked for LVMH.

What saves fashion mavens from the deepest sort of ridicule is that they don't take themselves too seriously. They seem to know how arbitrary their tastemaking is, and understand the absurdity of declaring one dress to be worth $10,000 and another to be worth $50. There's a certain tongue-in-cheek aspect to their attitude; they embrace the ridiculousness of their expert opinions.

As such, to lodge an exposé of the fashion industry's lack of substance would be to attack a straw man. I doubt that anybody who spends $10,000 on a dress is under the delusion that it's 2,000 times more attractive than something they could get at H&M. Rather, fashionistas seem to revel in the ridiculousness of the expenditure, in the arbitrariness of an of-the-moment anointment. They seem comfortable with the idea that *who*'s wearing something is more important than *what*'s being worn, and are comfortable with the idea that it's probably something that will go out of fashion next year and come back three decades hence. The fashion world is the very definition of self-conscious conspicuous consumption. It is what it is, and it knows what it is.

But wine can be, and should be, something more substantive than that. Even in contexts well beyond wine, there's a more personal element to putting something *inside* your body than putting something *on* your body, and since the days of Plato and Aristotle, it has been suggested that ideas more rigorous, scientific, and philosophical can emerge from the enterprise of creating, tasting, and thinking about wine. It was that sentiment that led

Alexandre Dumas to famously dub wine the "intellectual part" of the meal.

But when you consider the fact that rigorous blind tasting is still the exception in the world of wine ratings—and the rule is fuzzy, pretentious wine talk and a relentless drive toward proving to the world one's own ability to appreciate best what's most expensive—we wine enthusiasts start to look a lot more like the Champagne-guzzlers in Vegas than like the philosophers in Athens who looked toward wine for meditation, reflection, and self-exploration.

Chapter 5 So what?

Is there anything really wrong with this whole picture? Some interpreters of the evidence presented in this book have suggested that the placebo effect and conspicuous consumption are forms of consumer welfare that should be welcomed, not questioned. Apologists for the state of things have argued that when you buy a product, you are not just acquiring its physical usefulness; you're also purchasing what economists might call the "social utility" of being associated with the brand. You're buying into a perceived lifestyle, and it makes you happy.

"Conspicuous consumption and waste are an important part of social display," observes the *Economist* in an article about Plassmann and Rangel's work. "Deployed properly, they bring the rewards of status and better mating opportunities. For this to work, though, it helps if the displaying individual really believes that what he is buying is not only more expensive than the alternative, but better, too. Truly enjoying something simply because it is exclusive thus makes evolutionary sense."[23]

Moving on to the practical implications for the business world, the *Economist* points out that "Rangel's research also has implications for retailers, marketing firms and luxury-goods producers. It suggests that a successful marketing campaign can not only make people more interested in a product, but also, truly, make them enjoy it more."

Although the article does not specifically suggest that this would justify the value to the economy of those marketing campaigns, the implication seems to be there. That is, it wouldn't be much of a stretch to conclude that people's greater actual enjoyment of expensive goods once they know they're expensive *justifies*, from an economic standpoint, their high buy-in costs—and, by implication, their high marketing expenditures.

The fact that people like prestigious wine, in other words, means that the money that's been spent marketing its prestige has been spent *well*. It means that consumers benefit from all those good, expensive feelings exactly as they should, and nobody loses in the process. If $150 of pleasure is created by the combination of a marketing campaign and the $150 price tag itself, why should we mind? Can't we just dismiss this as a happy, if irrational, corner of the free market working properly?

Not in my view. When price alone can win over people's palates, winemakers lose their incentive to make wines that people would like if they were blind tasting—wines with *intrinsically* appealing qualities.

In spite of the fascinating new research that has been done in recent years, the neural underpinnings of the price effect are still ill understood. But, from a behavioral standpoint, I hypothesize that the price effect has a lot to do with attention: perhaps we simply pay more attention when we're drinking wine that we're told is expensive. We turn from passive drinkers to active drinkers. We keep the wine in our mouths longer, knowing that with each mouthful, we're swallowing away dollars, not cents. Our mind's eye investigates each of the wine's sensory properties, instead of drinking for simple enjoyment or easy inebriation. For a moment, we *give of ourselves*, and we get back more. Where we search for complexity, we find it. Where we seek beauty, it arises.

If we did that with every glass of wine we drank—not just the expensive ones—it would enable cheap wines to give us that expensive-wine experience. Not every bottle will do so, of course, but every bottle will have the *chance* to do so. To accept the premises of this book and pay real attention to every glass you drink is to shift the burden back onto the luxury producers to make a product that actually differentiates itself. Mere attention, perhaps, can set us free.

When consumers pay attention and liberate their palates from the placebo effect, wineries are forced compete to make better-tasting wines, and the bar of quality for the wine industry is raised. Competition on the merits raises the quality of *all* wines. It encourages producers whose wines give us little—even upon attention and reflection—to offer more.

But when wineries compete merely to market their wines more successfully, the consumer loses, because more resources go toward marketing, and fewer toward winemaking. A great winemaker is your friend, but one that substitutes marketing for winemaking is the enemy of the wine consumer. And a company that spends as much (or more) money on marketing as it does on research, development, and production—a company like LVMH—is delivering poor value to consumers. When we pay their premiums and fund their advertising campaigns, we are literally *paying them to tell us that we like their product.*

Marketing wasn't always about appealing to our social or emotional insecurities, and it wasn't always a waste of resources. Look at any pre-World War II magazine, and you'll see pages full of advertisements that actually discussed the substantive advantages of their products. For instance, a pair of shoes or a shirt would be advertised as having more durable soles or better fabric. That sort of advertising served an *informational* purpose: it informed the consumer about the product's availability and about the real differences between that product and others. It cast the product onto the consumer's radar screen, and the dissemination of that information helped the market function fluidly.

That's not what's going on when you see a wine associated with a scantily clad woman, a celebrity, or a kangaroo, or branded with a name like "Mommy's Time Out," "Four Emus," "Little Black Dress," or "Old Fart." What do these names have to do with wine? The information dissemination has been replaced by brands elbowing for emotional space in consumers' minds. Effective modern wine marketing is rarely about communicating the way the wine tastes or smells; it's more about communicating a lifestyle. It's about preying on our social needs—the same needs that drive our tendency toward conspicuous consumption—rather than our sensory ones.

In economic terms, the marketing of consumer products in the modern world is a zero-sum game. Every time a consumer chooses one sparkling wine over another based on marketing, and not on the results of blind tastings, the one company wins and another loses. But the money that both have spent competing on lifestyle marketing is wasted. For every winner, there's a loser. And since the consumer ultimately pays for the marketing, whoever wins, the consumer *always* loses.

The emergence of emotional marketing, and the accompanying replacement of true consumer choice with an opaque network of intermediaries and social forces, is hardly limited to the wine industry. Take cars, for instance. In the last gasps of the gilded age, even as General Motors was beginning to crumble, Cadillac turned into a fascinating study in modern marketing: on the verge of obsolescence, the company managed to reposition its image completely, from Eldorado to Escalade, turning itself from the canonical conspicuous-consumption emblem of Morty Seinfeld's generation into the canonical conspicuous-consumption emblem of Jay-Z's generation.

The still-not-quite-dead Cadillac brand launched a new motto, which you can still find scrawled across many of its highway billboard ads. It is simply this: "Life, liberty, and the pursuit."

Veblen would love it: "of happiness" has been cut from a phrase that has, for generations, been understood to embody the essence of the American spirit. Happiness, it seems, is no longer the point. It's just "the pursuit."

The pursuit of *what*?

Chapter 6 Critics and critiques

Blind tasting is not a one-sided issue. There has been some sophisticated discussion about its pros and cons. The *New York Times* wine writer Eric Asimov, in an interesting series of articles, has argued that blind tasting is insufficient as a way to judge wine. In his first such article, which came out before the first edition of this book, Asimov argues that "blind tastings eliminate knowledge and context that can be significant in judging a wine...I feel it's a little like judging a book by reading one chapter or one page."[24] Insisting on blind tasting—continues Asimov in his second post on the subject—prevents you from understanding the wine you're judging: "It's almost an anti-intellectual position. Obviously what's in the glass matters. But I think the more knowledge you can bring to a wine, the better your understanding of that wine will be."[25]

Asimov's part in this debate over the merits of blind tasting intensified after he responded on his blog to a *Newsweek* article about this book that came out in advance of its publication, and then again after having read the galleys. His writing on the subject culminated in a print article in the *Times*, which, along with the blog posts and lively exchange of reader comments, would make good reading for anyone interested in this book.[26, 27]

When positions become polarized, of course, the subtlety of each side's thought is muted, and straw men show up. I doubt, for instance, that Asimov really takes me to be arguing that wine writers shouldn't discuss the story behind a wine, that they shouldn't mention the pudding stones of Châteauneuf-du-Pape or the eccentricities of Josko Gravner and his amphorae. In fact, we discuss just those sorts of stories in the second half of this book, where we review wines. Our descriptions do not rely solely on blind tasting notes. Without a doubt, a lot of the fun of wine is in all the stuff that's *not* in the glass.

Indeed, to drink a wine blind with dinner, thus neutralizing all the sensory/emotional value we get from our brain's processing of the extrinsic facts about a wine—the same value that's demonstrated by the experiments cited in this book—would be the greatest folly of all. The intellectual enterprise of wine appreciation that Dumas described would be incomplete without knowing what wine one is thinking or talking about. In fact, if the wine is expensive, telling everyone how much it cost you—though gauche—might even help your guests enjoy it more.

The more interesting point that Asimov makes is about the artificiality of any blind-tasting experiment—first and foremost, about the fact that wine is meant to be drunk with food, and that it is inherently problematic to judge it in isolation. "I personally think wine is experienced in a different way," he writes, "when it's consumed with a meal over time, and that's one reason why, in this blog, I do not write about wines that I've only sipped in tastings." Asimov rails against "the mass-tasting environment," arguing that "it's a completely unnatural way to taste and to judge wine. Rather than drink wine in a natural environment with food, wines are pitted against each other, sipped and spit, one after another."

Most wine *is* better and more complex with food; there's no doubt about that. There's a fair argument to be made that when your goal is to maximize your sheer pleasure from wine, you should only drink it with food. Even terrible wine can taste good with the right food.

But to seriously *evaluate* wine together with food is to make a similar mistake as evaluating it non-blind: it confounds the results of an already unscientific process—the subjective sensory evaluation of wine—with dozens of other even less predictable variables.

It is true that information about your experience of a wine in the absence of food, or in a sequence of other wines, will not be perfectly relevant to a reader's future experience of that same wine over a relaxing meal. But information about how the wine's fruit character and tannins reacted with your next-door neighbor's demi-glace might well be even less relevant.

The more important problem with Asimov's general critique, though, is that to dismiss blind tasting as superficial is to sidestep the troubling realities of the current marketplace that blind tasting aims to address. The central problem in the wine world is not that too many wine critics aren't pairing wine with food, or that wine companies are turning out too many bottles.

The central problem is that wine pricing is almost completely arbitrary—that the price of wine does not significantly correlate to the pleasure it brings, *even to experts*.

It's that Robert Parker, *Wine Spectator*, and others with economic power in the industry are propping up the myth that price and pleasure *do* correlate strongly, that it really *is* possible that not one of 6,475 wines under $10 would score above 91. It's that generations of consumers are now growing up taking that myth as fact, and drinking and buying wine in a way that conforms to the myth.

Some of the biggest victims of this state of affairs are the very "artisanal, natural or hand-crafted categories" that Asimov so admires. Their livelihoods hang in the balance. Most of them learn, often through trial and error, that to get a truly high rating in (or even to be acknowledged by) most wine magazines, your wine must first be expensive; and to justify charging that much, you must make it in a certain style and hire a certain consultant; and before you know it, you've made not the wine you wanted to make, but rather the wine the magazine told you to make.

Of all the winemakers with whom I've spoken about this set of issues, I can't think of one that was comfortable with the power held by, or the reliability of, the institutions that assign point scores to wine. If there is a single issue that irks good, honest wine producers, it's the grip held on them by this network of corrupt-at-worst, highly-suggestible-at-best 100-point tastemakers; their junketeering; their blind reverence for the super-premium Screaming Eagle/Sassicaia/Pétrus/Vega Sicilia/Penfolds Grange hierarchy; and their affiliated ad-sales networks. Producers who are simply trying to make good wine and sell it at a fair price complain about this particular state of things even more than they complain about the unpredictability of the weather.

Perhaps some form of ratings—or at least recommendations—must exist, with or without food pairings. But it's inappropriate for a magazine's tasters—just before assigning an evaluative score that is likely to have a major impact on the wine's price, on its availability to everyday wine drinkers, and on the producer's financial well-being—to be told that the wine they're about to taste is a 2005 Pomerol, or (on the other end of the spectrum) a Merlot from Baja California.

In those cases, the placebo effect—which, as Brochet and Weil have shown, applies to experts just as it does to everyday wine drinkers—colors the evaluation: good wines from humble or stigmatized regions are penalized; average wines from famous, expensive regions are rewarded; and the chronic overrating and overpricing of prestige wines is perpetuated.

This is the vicious cycle of non-blind rating that has poisoned the modern wine industry. It is the cycle that has driven the release price of a good vintage of Pétrus to $5,000 per bottle, and it is the cycle that maintains the price of Dom Pérignon at $150. Everybody inside or outside the industry who knows better should speak out against the poisonous myth spread by so much of the wine establishment that while not every expensive wine must be great, every great wine must be expensive.

The aim of The Wine Trials—aside from seeking out good, widely available values under $15—is to question the institutional structures that govern the industry, to encourage people to learn their own palates through the exercise of tasting blind instead of trusting the numerical scores that Parker and the magazines assign. It is the economic power of these institutional structures that damages not only the wallet of the everyday consumer, but also the chances for a small, interesting, good-value producer—even one that makes wine costing more than $15—to succeed on the store shelf or on the restaurant wine list.

Anyone who seeks to defend those producers' prospects for success should join in and speak out against the pay-to-play schemes at the wine magazines and other publications whose main business is selling ads to the very wineries whose products they evaluate. Their incentives are twisted from the start, and there is enormous anecdotal evidence that even if an ad won't guarantee you a high rating, it will increase the chances that your wine will at least be reviewed in the publication—which, for smaller producers, is often the tougher battle. It is time for people who care about wine to hold the irresponsible critics accountable, because their market manipulations currently threaten the fabric of the industry.

As things stand, our society of wine drinkers—and consumers of other goods—rides on the placebo effect more than most people are willing to admit. My hope is that once you've begun tasting blind, the placebo effect will fade in favor of something better: the pleasure of enjoying a good wine at a good price—and a wine that you know is good, however little you might have paid.

Once you're choosing wine purely on its merits, you've taken away the power of lifestyle marketing, and you've enhanced your ability to find pleasure in an inexpensive bottle—and, for that matter, in an expensive one, too. You've become a real consumer.

Although glossy magazines might have you believe otherwise, the choice to buy a wine—or to buy anything else—on the reputation of a brand alone is a *sacrifice* of your individuality, not an expression of it. America is the country that spread free-market capitalism around the world, yet by accepting what we're told products are worth instead of determining their value for ourselves, we're turning our version of capitalism into something else. We're withdrawing the consumer's power to shape the demand curve that is meant to keep the market at equilibrium. In the swordfight of supply and demand, we're laying down our weapons and bowing before the supply curve, letting producers unilaterally tell us what we want—and at what price. That's not a healthy free market. That's LVMH's Five-Year Plan.

To be a skeptical consumer—to look past the tastemakers and magazines, to experience the liquid and judge wine on its pure underlying merits, and to learn about the wine while you're at it— is to flex the fingers of capitalism's invisible hand, to push the system to work the way that it is supposed to work.

But to surrender, instead, to the siren song of marketing and price signals—to buy what you're told to buy, or to assume that expensive means good—is to withdraw your own brain from free participation in our own market economy. It is not just self-destructive. It is, to me, un-American.

Chapter 7 The culture war

No man also having drunk old wine
straightway desireth new: for he saith,
The old is better.
                   –*King James Bible,* Luke 5:39

What is the purpose of wine? Is it meant to be served before
dinner, with dinner, or with dessert? Is it meant to be drunk in your
living room, on the beach, or at a world-class restaurant? The
answer to all of these questions is yes, and the answers to what
wine should taste like are different in each case.

Beyond that, though, one of the central themes of this book has
been that even when people are in controlled blind-tasting
settings—even when they are confronted with the exact same
wines as each other, in the exact same situations—there is often
not much agreement between them over which wines are best.

There are the New World wine lovers and the Old World wine
lovers; there are the fruit-and-oak lovers and the earth-and-mineral
lovers; and there is everything in between. There are people who
love Australian Shiraz with sushi on the beach, and people who
will drink Sancerre in front of the fireplace on a cold winter's night.
I have seen a group of Hong Kong businessmen mix 1970 Château

Latour with Coca-Cola before drinking it. People's preferences in wine vary wildly, even within the ranks of those that have gone through extensive training.

When you figure in genetic differences, differences in upbringing, differences in understanding about what purpose wine is supposed to serve, and differences in mood or body chemistry on a given day or at a given moment, blind tasting data become so noisy that one needs to collect thousands of data points to get any statistically significant results at all. This is true even when the tasters are all experienced wine professionals. "Variation in judgment, even among experts," write Amerine and Roessler, "is why we reject single-judge evaluations."

Yet amidst this culture war, the world of wine criticism is coming to be dominated by exactly those types of single-judge evaluations. Amidst all this instability and dissent in the wine world, there is one relatively sure thing: that as the global industry modernizes its equipment and winemaking style, it is converging on one stylistic direction, one basic taste profile. Many expensive wines seem to have mastered that style; inexpensive wines are emulating it everywhere; and the style is catching on all around the world, even in traditionally non-wine-drinking countries.

The style is specific, it's easily identifiable, and it is more commonly found in wines made by modern producers from the New World (e.g. the United States and Australia) than wines made by traditional producers from the Old World (e.g. France, Spain, Portugal, and Italy), although this is rapidly changing.[28] The single most recognizable aspect of the style is that it plays to the world's sweet tooth.

Proponents of the modern New World style tend to describe it with words like jammy, fruit-forward, big, full-bodied, and concentrated. Opponents complain that New World methods create similar wines, regardless of the region, resulting in a convergence of the world's wine styles and a loss of diversity.

Then there is the Old World style, whose proponents like to talk about it as balanced, elegant, sometimes austere, and, at its best, faithfully representative of a particular terroir (the unique characteristics of a region's geography, climate, soil, and so on). Old World wine often takes more time to mature than does New World wine.

You may fall upon either side of the divide; there's certainly no shame in liking concentrated New World fruit, or in disliking Old World acidity, dustiness, and minerality. What's hard to debate, though, is that the New World style is currently winning the race by a landslide. The runaway success of the Australian wine brand Yellow Tail—whose Chardonnay and Shiraz are now the world's two best-selling wines, each selling more than 20 million bottles per year—is evidence enough of that, as is the fact that even famous, centuries-old Old World wines, including first-growth Bordeaux, are slowly converting to the New World style.

It has become quite fashionable in food and wine circles to blame (or thank, depending on your perspective) Robert Parker for all of this. The influence of the world's most famous wine critic is powerful indeed. But, as has been discussed above, not everybody likes Parker's palate, and it's also fashionable in certain circles (especially the restaurant industry), to hate Parker and his "big, dumb wines."

Setting aside Parker himself, though, it is indisputable that this style of wine is appealing to an increasing percentage of wine drinkers, and the reasons for this are probably more related to our collective upbringing than to anything else.

Just as your taste and smell experience can change at a moment's notice when you think you're drinking an expensive wine, your experience can change over time as you acquire preferences for new or different tastes and smells; in psychology and neuroscience, this phenomenon is known as perceptual learning. Most of us have experienced some version of it as we've grown up. Maybe you didn't like mushrooms or blue cheese when you were a little kid, for instance—and maybe you didn't like wine at all the first time you tried it. (You presumably do now, if you've read this far.)

One thing that kids almost universally like is sugar, and our culture has become uniquely indulgent of that taste. People make a big deal about how American children are growing up on fast food, but at least fast food, for the most part, tastes good. However unhealthy a McDonald's Quarter Pounder with Cheese is, and however suspect the provenance of its ingredients, the burger is well seasoned and has a reasonable balance of tastes and textures. What's totally out of balance, though, is the flavor profile of soft drinks. All health concerns aside, sugar is the silent killer of our nation's palate.

Children are building up such an early tolerance for sweet things, and in terms of gustatory tolerance, artificial sweeteners are just as bad as sugar. That sweetness has started to dominate the taste of foods whose traditional recipes don't even call for sugar, such as salad dressing.

As a result, when, as adults, they start drinking wine, they don't even perceive the likes of Yellow Tail as sweet. Wine industry consultant Jon Fredrikson, in an interview with the *New York Times*, has called Yellow Tail "the perfect wine for a public grown up on soft drinks."[29]

Perhaps, then, it shouldn't be surprising that Robert Parker has called the Yellow Tail wines "surprisingly well-made": he, too, grew up on soft drinks. According to Elin McCoy, his biographer, Parker hadn't had a single glass of dry wine until he was 20 years old, on his first trip to France: "Since Coca-Cola was so expensive, a dollar for a tiny bottle, Pat [his girlfriend] insisted he try *un verre du vin*, the first dry wine Parker had ever tasted."[30]

In other words, the culprit for the style convergence might not be Parker himself, or his followers themselves; it might be the taste for sugar that he, and they, all acquired in childhood—a taste that an increasing percentage of the world's children are also now acquiring.

Certainly Parker's rise can be attributed in part to his charisma, his business acumen, his consistent palate, his writing style, and many other factors—but it also might be attributed in part to the fact that people who grew up with a sweet tooth feel vindicated by Parker's palate.

As wine continues to spread to vast swaths of the world whose populations have scarcely encountered it outside of elite hotels— China, Africa, Southeast Asia, India—the natural first tendency is the child's instinct: to go for what's sweet, or at least fruity. And we see the same happening in the swaths of our own country that aren't as steeped in wine tradition—the rural Midwest, the deep South. Could it be that the Parkerization of the world's wine industry owes less to Parker himself, and more to the expansion of the economic pie that free trade and globalization have enabled?

Should we call Yellow Tail not "Parkerized," but rather "globalized"?

Whether or not you find the globalized style pleasant on a sensory level, a more fundamental problem is that it's a style of wine that's not created by nature, but rather by aggressive intervention with techniques like aging wine in new oak barrels for extended periods of time. What's even more bothersome, though, is the fact that, driven by the ratings of Parker and his progeny, the worlds of cheap and expensive wines all over the world seem to be converging on a single taste profile. As globalized wine is being introduced even to Rioja, the traditional style that has produced unique local wines in those regions is being replaced with one common "international" style that's geared toward getting high scores from magazine critics like Parker and *Wine Spectator*. And we've seen in the previous chapter how much those high scores matter.

As the world's wines grow more similar to each other with each successive vintage, the incredible diversity of the world's wine regions is being lost, and—perhaps due to undue deference to the magazine critics' ratings—the world's high-end wine consumers are supporting the trend with their wallets.

Whatever style of wine you *think* you like, you owe it to yourself, and to the wine world, to test that assumption scientifically. Either way, it's important that you make sure you *agree* with the magazine critics, at least, before jumping onto the New World bandwagon.

Maybe for *you*, a bottle of Dom Pérignon, Screaming Eagle, or Château Pétrus really is worth the $150, $2,000, or $5,000 that it commands. Either way, once you've decided for yourself— firsthand and blind, with only your palate in charge—whether or not the Emperor is dressed, your brain's curious habit of making things taste like you expect them to taste—of making expensive things taste better, and of making cheap things taste worse— might lessen, too.

That's the funny thing about our brains, and about expectations. If this book makes you skeptical of high price tags, just reading it could change the taste of expensive wine for you. What will change your experience even more, though, is blind tasting yourself. By questioning wine prices, you will become less of a slave to expectations and more of a student of your own palate. Invoking only the simple, everyday miracle of the scientific method, you will have turned a placebo into wine.

Chapter 8 Drinking games for adults

To try your hand at blind tasting, you don't need to be as obsessive-compulsive as we were when putting together this book. At home, or even at a BYO restaurant, it's fairly easy to blind taste a few wines at a time.

You don't need much to start. Tasting forms for everyday wine drinkers can be downloaded from thewinetrials.com. Brown lunch bags from the supermarket work well to conceal wines, and packing tape does a decent job of sealing them in. Champagne buckets, beach pails, large plastic tumblers, or cocktail shakers will all work as spit buckets; even if you don't plan to spit, you'll need buckets for dumping out remaining wine between tastes.

Beyond that, the key ingredients are wine, lots of paper, pens, patient friends, and matching glasses. (Differently shaped glasses can have different effects on the wine, although this effect has been grossly exaggerated by glassware companies.)

However many wines you want to taste, split your wines into flights to two to six bottles each. Palate fatigue can set in when you hit the seventh or eighth wine, and it's also difficult to rank wines against each other when more than six are involved.

If you're using standard wine glasses, then be sure, at a minimum, that your glasses curve inward at the top and aren't merely cylindrical. But the ideal glasses for blind tasting are 155 mm ISO tasting glasses, designed by scientists in France to concentrate the aromas at exactly the point where your nose sticks into the glass. They're small enough to fit many on a table, and their tapered shape is also designed to allow for vigorous swirling without spillage. These are the glasses used in many wine industry conventions and fairs, and they are what we used in our blind tastings. You can order ISO-certified tasting glasses at thewinetrials.com.

If you're doing an informal tasting at a party, there are really only four important rules to keep in mind: first, remove the entire foil top on the wine, not just the top of it, as you might normally. Foil can be a dead giveaway. Second, the person who bagged and sealed the wines (with the packing tape around the neck) shouldn't be the same person who numbers the bottles (a Sharpie works best). Third, once the tasting begins, tasters shouldn't be allowed to discuss wines with each other before assigning their ratings—that will introduce serious bias toward the opinions of the more self-confident people in the group. Finally, tasters shouldn't be allowed to change their ratings after the wines have been exposed. That would defeat the whole purpose of the game. Of course, it goes without saying that tasters shouldn't be told *anything* about the wine they're tasting beforehand—not even the country of origin or grape, and certainly not the price range.

If you want to do a more formal tasting, there are several other things you should keep in mind. First, you should transfer screwcap wines into empty non-screwcap bottles to avoid bias, because the threads will be visible even after the wine is brown-bagged. Magnums, jug wines, and box wines should also be transferred to normal 750 mL bottles in the same way.

Unless you're tasting older vintages, wines should be left uncorked for a minimum of 45 minutes before serving to let them breathe and minimize oxygen reduction that can taint wine aromas, particularly with screwcap wines. White wines should be tasted at around 55°F to 60°F (13°C to 16°C), somewhat above the temperature at which you would normally drink them; it's easier to tell the difference between wines when they're warmer. In general, taking whites from the refrigerator, opening them, and leaving them to breathe at room temperature for about 30 minutes should do the trick. Red wines should be tasted around 60°F to 65°F (16°C to 18°C).

With respect to pouring wines, there are two methods that work, depending on how many glasses you have. The method that best allows for wine-against-wine comparison is to distribute one glass for each wine to each taster, and to pour all the wines at once. So if you had four tasters and six wines, you'd need 24 glasses. (If you don't have a dishwasher, you'll hate this method.)

The second method, which is more suitable for large numbers of people, is to give the tasters one glass each and let them pour wines themselves as they go. In that case, after tasting each wine, tasters should rinse their glasses with the next wine to be tasted before pouring the actual tasting portion. When rinsing, tasters should make an effort to coat the whole inside surface of the glass with the new wine while holding the glass upside down over the spit bucket and slowly pouring it out. Once the glass is coated, tasters can then pour a full tasting portion of the next wine.

When the wines are served, every taster should be given a rating form and a pen. Serve plain water crackers (Carr's plain flavor is reliably neutral) at the table to cleanse the palate between wines. Some people like to drink water between wines as well, although it's not as good a palate cleanser as crackers.

Encourage tasters to pour two-ounce tasting portions, to take at most one swallow of each wine, and to spit on repeated tastes. (Very few people will get wasted on six swallows of wine, and some people—I'm on the fence—feel that something is lost on the finish if you don't swallow at least once.) If tasters are tempted to drink more than that, remind them that once the tasting is finished and the bottles are exposed, they can drink as much as they want.

Encourage your tasters to taste the wines in random order. It's well established that tasters have a positive bias towards the first item tasted or rated in a series, and in our tastings we took steps to ensure that tasters did not all taste in the same order.

Tasters should both rate and rank the wines. Ranking is a more accurate way of scoring wines *against each other*, because it forces tasters to make tough decisions, but rating is the best way to compare wines from one flight or tasting to wines from another. Our rating scale is intentionally simple, and we have four rating check boxes—as opposed to five—so that tasters are forced to make the tough decision between the second and third, rather than falling back on an indecisive middle choice. Accordingly, you should not allow tasters to check between boxes.

When all the tasters are done rating, make it clear that people are no longer allowed to make changes to their forms, and then, with great fanfare and drama, expose the wines. Don't forget to immediately record which wine corresponds to which bag number. The simplest way of scoring the wines is called a "rank sum": you add up all the tasters' rankings, and the lowest score wins. To calculate a total *rating*, count one point for every bad vote, two for okay, three for good, four for great, and the highest score wins.

And remember, above all else, that even a taster under the influence of alcohol is better than a taster under the influence of others—or of the label.

Notes on Part I

1. Winning wines from the previous edition of *The Wine Trials* were grandfathered into the tastings, allowing them to bypass the nomination process and defend their titles regardless of this year's case production numbers or whether they were re-nominated by industry professionals. Once entered into the blind tastings, though, these previous winners received no special consideration.

2. Economists often use logarithmic price scales to analyze wine pricing, as we did; this helps to test the hypothesis that a wine's price might increase exponentially as its quality increases linearly.

3. Some people in the wine industry dispute the validity of tasting cheap wines against expensive wines, objecting that the former are generally easier to enjoy on their own, while the latter need to be served with food and/or need to age for several years. See Chapter 7 for a discussion on the question of reviewing wine paired with food. However, controlled wine tastings have long been the accepted industry standard for the evaluation of wines at any price range. As for the question of age, older vintages of expensive wines are rarely available at most wine stores or restaurants, so they would not properly represent the wines people are actually

buying and drinking. Tasting older wines would also increase the likelihood of many other confounding factors, including improper storage, oxidation, and cork taint.

4. Robin Goldstein, Johan Almenberg, Anna Dreber, Alexis Herschkowitsch, and Jacob Katz, "Do More Expensive Wines Taste Better? Evidence from a Large Sample of US Blind Tastings," *Journal of Wine Economics,* Vol. 3, No. 1 (Spring 2008).

5. Jancis Robinson, *Confessions of a Wine Lover* (Penguin Books, 1997).

6. Maynard Amerine and Edward Roessler, *Wines: Their Sensory Evaluation* (W.H. Freeman and Company, 1976).

7. Sébastien Lecocq and Michael Visser, "What Determines Wine Prices: Objective vs. Sensory Characteristics," *Journal of Wine Economics*, Vol. 1, No. 1 (Spring 2006).

8. When I refer to "Champagne," I mean only wines that come from the French Champagne appellation, which are rarely available for less than $25 and are often far more expensive than that.

9. Frédéric Brochet, "Chemical Object Representation in the Field of Consciousness" (application presented for the Grand Prix of the Académie Amorim following work carried out towards a doctorate from the Faculty of Oenology of Bordeaux, General Oenology Laboratory), 2001.

10. Ralph Allison and Kenneth Uhl, "Influence of Beer Brand Identification on Taste Perception," *Journal of Marketing Research,* Vol. 1, No. 3 (August 1964).

11. Leonard Lee, Shane Frederick, and Dan Ariely, "Try It, You'll Like It: The Influence of Expectation, Consumption, and Revelation on Preferences for Beer," *Psychological Science*, Vol. 17, No. 12 (December 2006).

12. Johan Almenberg and Anna Dreber, "When Does the Price Affect the Taste? Results from a Wine Experiment," Stockholm

School of Economics Working Paper in Economics and Finance No. 717 (August 2009).

13. Hilke Plassmann, John O'Doherty, Baba Shiv, and Antonio Rangel, "Marketing Actions Can Modulate Neural Representations of Experienced Pleasantness," *Proceedings of the National Academy of Sciences* (January 14, 2008), http://www.pnas.org/cgi/content/abstract/0/06929105v1.

14. Statistics were taken from custom searches for wines $10 and under from the 2000 to 2007 vintages performed on both www.winespectator.com (subscribers only) and www.wineenthusiast.com (open to the public). 1,953 wines returned by the *Wine Enthusiast* search with prices listed as $0 were ignored.

15. Roman Weil, "Analysis of Reserve and Regular Bottlings: Why Pay for a Difference Only the Critics Claim to Notice?" *Chance*, Vol. 18, No. 3 (Summer 2005).

16. Tyler Colman, Dr. Vino blog, "Changes at the *Wine Advocate*? Correspondence with Parker and Miller," http://www.drvino.com/2009/04/16/changes-at-the-wine-advocate-correspondence-with-parker-and-miller (April 16, 2009).

17. Robin Goldstein, Blind Taste blog, "What Does It Take To Get a Wine Spectator Award of Excellence?", http://blindtaste.com/2008/08/15/what-does-it-take-to-get-a-wine-spectator-award-of-excellence (August 15, 2008).

18. James Laube, Laube Untined Blog, "When Tasting, Blind Offers Vision," www.winespectator.com/Wine/Blogs/Blog_Detail/0,4211,1426,00.html (October 4, 2007).

19. The website is not clear on how specific the regions or appellations with which *Wine Spectator* critics are provided prior to tasting, so I don't know if they're told the wine is from its specific appellation, "Hermitage," or the more general region "Northern Rhône." However, Hermitage is listed on Spectator's wine review search page as one of the "Wine Regions," so it seems reasonable to assume that it fits into their definition of "region."

20. LVMH 2007 Annual Report, available online at http://www.lvmh.com/comfi/pdf_gbr/LVMH2007AnnualReport.pdf.

21. Constellation 2007 Annual Report, available online at http://library.corporate-ir.net/library/85/851/85116/items/252600/STZ_2007AR.pdf.

22. Justin Weinberg, "Taste How Expensive This Is," in *Wine & Philosophy: A Symposium on Thinking and Drinking*, ed. Fritz Allhoff (Blackwell Publishing, 2008).

23. "Hitting the spot," *The Economist*, January 17, 2008.

24. Eric Asimov, The Pour, "If I Only Knew When I Tasted It…" http://thepour.blogs.nytimes.com/2007/09/13/if-i-only-knew-when-i-tasted-it/ (September 13, 2007).

25. Eric Asimov, The Pour, "Judging the Judging," http://thepour.blogs.nytimes.com/2007/09/17/judging-the-judging/ (September 17, 2007).

26. Eric Asimov, The Pour, "A Closer Look at 'The Wine Trials,'" http://http://thepour.blogs.nytimes.com/2008/04/22/a-closer-look-at-the-wine-trials/ (April 22, 2008).

27. Eric Asimov, "Wine's Pleasures: Are They All In Your Head?" *New York Times*, May 7, 2008.

28. The "New World" designation also traditionally includes wines from Chile, Argentina, New Zealand, and South Africa, and the "Old World" designation generally includes all of Europe.

29. Frank J. Prial, "The Wallaby That Roared Across the Wine Industry," *New York Times* (April 23, 2006).

30. Elin McCoy, *The Emperor of Wine: The Rise of Robert M. Parker, Jr., and the Reign of American Taste* (Ecco, 2005).

Part II The 2010 Wine Trials
by Alexis Herschkowitsch
with Tyce Walters

Chapter 9 About the 2010 trials

In the pages that follow, the *Wine Trials* editors review the 150 winners of this year's Wine Trials—the top-scoring wines under $15 from our brown-bag blind tastings of the new releases for 2010. (For more on our selection process, please see the preface.)

The United States is the most represented region in the book, with 54 of the 150 winners, of which 45 are from California, eight are from Washington State, and sadly, only one—Erath Pinot Gris—is from Oregon. (Unfortunately, Willamette Valley Pinot Noir, one of America's most reliable appellations, rarely dips below $15.)

We've been delighted by the more balanced style of this year's California Chardonnays, especially the surprising Fetzer Valley Oaks—a wine long known for being a cheap oak bomb that has redefined itself with bright acidity. Strong showings also came from a rich Geyser Peak Cabernet Sauvignon; the Black Box Cabernet Sauvignon, which continues to redefine the box-wine genre, and Washington State's Domaine Ste. Michelle Brut, which beat the $150 Dom Pérignon head to head for the second year in a row.

Perhaps the biggest regional surprise this year came from Portugal, which boasted a surprising 12 *Wine Trials* winners, from sprightly, summery, staggeringly inexpensive Vinho Verde to some complex, inky bottles from the Alentejo region. Argentina also turned in an extremely strong performance, with 21 wines in the top 150, headlined by an unprecedented four wines from Norton, our 2010 Winery of the Year. Argentine producers seem to have discovered a more delicate winemaking style, returning to their earthy, peppery roots and moving a bit away from the fruit-forward international style that recently swept through the region.

Spain was another success story, with 15 wines in the top 150, of which eight were from the earthy, old-school region of Rioja. Four Spanish wines made the finals, including the flowery, mulchy, endlessly seductive LAN Crianza, our Wine of the Year for 2010.

France and Italy held their own, with 15 and 17 winners, respectively, although both were hurt by higher prices owing to the strong euro; some of the top scorers from last year, like the crisp and wonderful Feudi di San Gregorio Falanghina from Italy's Campania region, were disqualified after crossing above the $15 barrier. Unfortunately, there was only one winner from Austria and one from Germany, also due to so many of the wines being priced out of our range this year—we'd love to see more under-$15 availability from those underappreciated wine regions.

There were some losing regions, too. For all the fanfare about good value from Australia, that country's wines did terribly in our tastings for the second edition in a row, with only three wines in our top 150 in spite of many nominations. South African wines did even worse, without a single winner. In both of these cases, blind tasters complained about a "burnt rubber" or "forest fire" character in many of the reds; an over-the-top sweetness or fruit-forwardness in both reds and whites; and a general lack of balance between fruit and acidity. The whack-you-over-the-head winemaking style that began in America seems to have moved its epicenter to these Southern Hemisphere regions, while back in the States, we've finally learned to rein it in a bit.

Of course, if you've taken this book seriously so far, then you'll take our blind tasting results with a grain of salt. To some extent, these choices might reflect the preferences of wine experts more than those of wine novices, as the *Wine Trials* editors all have plenty of experience with wine. (That said, tasters for the final round, in which the "Best of the Wine Trials" winners were chosen, were a mix of experts and everyday wine drinkers.)

It bears mention that there are many excellent values under $15 from smaller producers that unfortunately did not meet our criteria for widespread availability. That's why it's doubly important to work toward creating your own top 100. In a sophisticated wine store, the best place to start is often with the wines you *haven't* heard of—not because wines from obscure regions or producers are necessarily *better*, but because you're not paying a premium for a name-brand region or producer. A good wine store employee can be more helpful than a magazine critic. But nothing can substitute for taking the wine home and blind-tasting it yourself against other wines.

You'll notice that, unlike the rest of the book, the reviews are written in first-person plural ("we"); that's because they represent a joint effort between Robin Goldstein, Alexis Herschkowitsch, Tyce Walters, and the rest of our 17-member editorial blind tasting panel. In general, we tried to highlight sensory notes that were shared by multiple blind tasters, not just one taster's flight of fancy, although the latter was sometimes so amusing that we couldn't help ourselves. (Some good comments didn't make it in the book because the wine didn't qualify, like one taster's succinct description of Sutter Home White Zinfandel: "If Jesus tasted this wine, he'd turn it back to water.")

After the wines were revealed, we also added non-blind portions of review text discussing the producer, grapes, bottle design, and so on; but we did not change any tasting notes or descriptions, nor did we change any decisions about which wines would be included.

"Heavy" vs. "light" is a subjective distinction, to be sure, but one we hope you'll get used to; roughly speaking, it corresponds with alcohol content, thickness of texture, intensity of flavor, and what wine people call "body," but that doesn't fully capture the distinction. There are also special categories for rosé, sparkling wines, and sweet or aromatic wines.

In our reviews, we've tried to use everyday language to describe the wines—adjectives that will make sense to everyday wine drinkers. We do use fruit flavors, of course; the English language doesn't really have any way of describing taste sensations without making reference to other taste sensations, the way it does for colors. But we've done our best to stick to familiar flavors. We'll talk about orange or grapefruit, not gooseberry or pencil lead.

The only two wine buzzwords that we use consistently are "tannins" and "acidity." Tannins are the quality (found only in red wines) that dry out the mouth; acidity is the opposite, the quality that makes your mouth water. We also review the design of each bottle—after all, as this book has shown, that's a big part of what you're buying. The average retail price in the book is found in a circle in the upper right-hand corner of the page. A white circle means a white wine, a red circle means a red wine, and a gray circle means a rosé. Sparkling wines have bubbles coming out of a white circle. Each review page also specifies the wine's region, vintage tasted, suggested food pairings (which are utterly subjective, of course), and grape varieties.

Speaking of grape varieties, you might be wondering why we don't categorize wines on that axis, as many wine guides do. There's a reason for this: our view is that, especially for inexpensive wines, categorization by grape variety can often be misleading and unhelpful. Certainly, in some cases, varieties do influence the taste of the wine—especially extremely acidic grapes like Sauvignon Blanc, or sweet or aromatic grapes like Muscat or Gewürztraminer—but in inexpensive wines, this effect is often minimal compared with the Old World-New World divide or the light-heavy style divide. For example, a Merlot from Bordeaux would probably tend to taste more like a Cabernet Sauvignon from Bordeaux than like a Merlot from the United States. (If you're unconvinced by this argument, you can look wines up by grape variety in the index beginning on page 220.)

Even if you do not agree with all of our selections, we hope that our results will serve, at least, as a useful starting point for your own blind tasting journey. We also hope you'll question your assumptions about wine pricing, hold blind-tasting parties with your friends, and ultimately, join us in helping to restore the kind of order to the market that might only come from a grassroots movement of consumers that make a conscious decision to trust their own palates more than price tags.

Chapter 10 Winners of the 2010 trials

2010 Wine of the year	Country	Price
LAN Rioja Crianza	Spain	$12

2010 Winery of the year		
Bodegas Norton	Argentina	

Best of the Wine Trials winners	Country	Price
Sparkling Domaine Ste. Michelle Brut	USA (WA)	$12
Light white Aveleda Fonte Vinho Verde	Portugal	$7
Heavy white Fetzer Chardonnay	USA (CA)	$9
Rosé Parallèle 45 Rosé	France	$13
Light red LAN Rioja Crianza	Spain	$12
Heavy red Geyser Peak Cabernet Sauvignon	USA (CA)	$15
Sweet/aromatic Clean Slate Riesling	Germany	$11

Best of the Wine Trials finalists	Country	Price
Black Box Cabernet Sauvignon *heavy red*	USA (CA)	$5
Bogle Pinot Noir *light red*	USA (CA)	$13
Campo Viejo Rioja Crianza *light red*	Spain	$11
Casal Garcia Vinho Verde *light white*	Portugal	$9
Casteller Cava *sparkling*	Spain	$13
Castello Monaci Pilùna *heavy red*	Italy	$12
Château Ste. Michelle Sauv. Blanc *light white*	USA (WA)	$9

continues on next page

Best of the Wine Trials finalists continued	Country	Price
Concannon Pinot Noir *light red*	USA (CA)	$15
Conquista Torrontés *sweet/aromatic*	Argentina	$9
Domaine Ste. Michelle Extra Dry *sparkling*	USA (WA)	$12
Don Miguel Gascón Malbec *heavy red*	Argentina	$12
El Coto de Rioja Crianza *light red*	Spain	$12
Freixenet Cordon Negro Extra Dry *sparkling*	Spain	$9
Guigal Côtes du Rhône *heavy red*	France	$13
Kourtaki Mavrodaphne *sweet/aromatic*	Greece	$10
Norton Malbec *heavy red*	Argentina	$11
Pascual Toso Sauvignon Blanc *light white*	Argentina	$13
Robert Mondavi Pinot Noir *light red*	USA (CA)	$11

Best bargains	Country	Price
Alice White Chardonnay *heavy white*	Australia	$7
Almaden Chardonnay *light white*	USA (CA)	$3
Aveleda Fonte Vinho Verde *light white*	Portugal	$7
Barefoot Pinot Grigio *light white*	USA (CA)	$7
Barefoot Merlot *heavy red*	USA (CA)	$7
Barefoot Zinfandel *heavy red*	USA (CA)	$7
Black Box Cabernet Sauvignon *heavy red*	USA (CA)	$5
Block No. 45 Petite Sirah *heavy red*	USA (CA)	$7
Charles Shaw Chardonnay *heavy white*	USA (CA)	$3
Charles Shaw Cabernet Sauvignon *heavy red*	USA (CA)	$3
CK Mondavi Chardonnay *heavy white*	USA (CA)	$7
Crane Lake Chardonnay *sweet/aromatic*	USA (CA)	$7
Crane Lake Pinot Grigio *sweet/aromatic*	USA (CA)	$7
Fish Eye Cabernet Sauvignon *heavy red*	USA (CA)	$6
Fuzelo Vinho Verde *light white*	Portugal	$7
Nathanson Creek Merlot *light red*	USA (CA)	$6
Paul Valmer Merlot *light red*	France	$5
René Barbier Mediterranean White *light white*	Spain	$6
Twin Vines Vinho Verde *light white*	Portugal	$7

All *Wine Trials 2010* winners

Sparkling	Country	Price
Casteller Cava	Spain	$13
Domaine Ste. Michelle Brut	USA (WA)	$12
Domaine Ste. Michelle Extra Dry	USA (WA)	$12
Freixenet Cordon Negro Brut	Spain	$9
Freixenet Cordon Negro Extra Dry	Spain	$9
Pirovano Prosecco	Italy	$15

Sparkling *continued*	*Country*	*Price*
Presto Prosecco	Italy	$10
Segura Viudas Brut Reserva	Spain	$8

Light Old World white	*Country*	*Price*
Aveleda Fonte Vinho Verde	Portugal	$7
Aveleda Vinho Verde	Portugal	$9
Casal Garcia Vinho Verde	Portugal	$9
Château Bonnet White	France	$13
Domäne Wachau Grüner Veltliner	Austria	$15
Fuzelo Vinho Verde	Portugal	$7
Marqués de Cáceres White Rioja	Spain	$10
Mezzacorona Chardonnay	Italy	$9
Mezzacorona Pinot Grigio	Italy	$10
Monte Velho White	Portugal	$8
ÖKO White	Italy	$10
René Barbier Mediterranean White	Spain	$6
Twin Vines Vinho Verde	Portugal	$7

Heavy Old World white	*Country*	*Price*
Cave de Lugny Mâcon-Villages	France	$11
Fat Bastard Chardonnay	France	$12
Le Grand Noir White	France	$10

Light New World white	*Country*	*Price*
Almaden Chardonnay	USA (CA)	$3
Barefoot Pinot Grigio	USA (CA)	$7
Château Ste. Michelle Pinot Gris	USA (WA)	$13
Château Ste. Michelle Sauvignon Blanc	USA (WA)	$9
Crane Lake Pinot Grigio	USA (CA)	$7
Erath Pinot Gris	USA (OR)	$15
Fetzer Sauvignon Blanc	USA (CA)	$9
Forest Glen Pinot Grigio	USA (CA)	$15
Francis Ford Coppola Bianco	USA (CA)	$11
Geyser Peak Sauvignon Blanc	USA (CA)	$14
Gnarly Head Pinot Grigio	USA (CA)	$11
Nobilo Sauvignon Blanc	New Zealand	$14
Oyster Bay Sauvignon Blanc	New Zealand	$13
Pascual Toso Sauvignon Blanc	Argentina	$13
Rock Rabbit Sauvignon Blanc	USA (CA)	$10
Rodney Strong Sauvignon Blanc	USA (CA)	$15
Saint Clair Sauvignon Blanc	New Zealand	$15
Santa Ema Sauvignon Blanc	Chile	$10

Heavy New World white

	Country	Price
Santa Rita 120 Sauvignon Blanc	Chile	$8
35° South Sauvignon Blanc	Chile	$9
Villa Maria Sauvignon Blanc	New Zealand	$15
Alice White Chardonnay	Australia	$7
Bonterra Chardonnay	USA (CA)	$14
Charles Shaw Chardonnay	USA (CA)	$3
CK Mondavi Chardonnay	USA (CA)	$7
Crane Lake Chardonnay	USA (CA)	$7
Fetzer Chardonnay	USA (CA)	$9
Hess Chardonnay	USA (CA)	$11
Pascual Toso Chardonnay	Argentina	$13
Santa Ema Chardonnay	Chile	$10
Santa Julia Chardonnay	Argentina	$11

Rosé

	Country	Price
El Coto de Rioja Rosado	Spain	$10
Parallèle 45 Rosé	France	$13

Light Old World red

	Country	Price
Caldora Montepulciano d'Abruzzo	Italy	$11
Campo Viejo Rioja Crianza	Spain	$11
Campo Viejo Rioja Reserva	Spain	$13
Castello di Querceto Chianti DOCG	Italy	$10
Charamba Douro	Portugal	$8
Château Bonnet Red	France	$15
Cortijo Rioja	Spain	$10
El Coto de Rioja Crianza	Spain	$12
Lan Rioja Crianza	Spain	$12
Le Grand Noir Pinot Noir	France	$10
Louis Latour Le Pinot Noir	France	$15
Manyana Tempranillo	Spain	$8
Melini Chianti San Lorenzo	Italy	$12
Montecillo Rioja Crianza	Spain	$12
Paul Valmer Merlot	France	$5
Pirovano Barbera	Italy	$10
Pirovano Sangiovese di Romagna	Italy	$9
Pisato Montepulciano d'Abruzzo	Italy	$13
Ruffino Aziano Chianti Classico	Italy	$15
Santa Cristina	Italy	$12
Straccali Chianti	Italy	$10
Vitiano (Falesco)	Italy	$9

Heavy Old World red

	Country	Price
Altano Douro	Portugal	$8
Arancio Stemmari Nero d'Avola	Italy	$9
Berco do Infante	Portugal	$8
Cabriz Red	Portugal	$11
Castello Monaci Pilùna	Italy	$12
Guigal Côtes du Rhône	France	$13
La Vieille Ferme Rouge	France	$8
Le Grand Noir GSM	France	$10
Ludovicus DO Terra Alta	Spain	$11
Monte da Cal	Portugal	$10
Mouton Cadet Bourdeaux Rouge	France	$10
ÖKO Red	France	$10
Parallèle 45 Rouge	France	$13
Quinta do Encontro	Portugal	$11

Light New World red

	Country	Price
Bogle Pinot Noir	USA (CA)	$13
Casa Silva Carménère Reserve	Chile	$13
Concannon Pinot Noir	USA (CA)	$15
Hahn Estates Pinot Noir	USA (CA)	$15
Mark West Pinot Noir	USA (CA)	$11
Nathanson Creek Merlot	USA (CA)	$6
Robert Mondavi Pinot Noir	USA (CA)	$11

Heavy New World red

	Country	Price
Alamos Malbec	Argentina	$10
Barefoot Merlot	USA (CA)	$7
Barefoot Zinfandel	USA (CA)	$7
Beringer Cabernet Sauvignon	USA (CA)	$11
Black Box Cabernet Sauvignon	USA (CA)	$5
Block #45 Petite Sirah	USA (CA)	$7
Bogle Cabernet Sauvignon	USA (CA)	$11
Bogle Old Vine Zinfandel	USA (CA)	$11
Bus Stop Red	Argentina	$10
Charles Shaw Cabernet Sauvignon	USA (CA)	$3
Columbia Crest Two Vines Shiraz	USA (WA)	$8
Concannon Petite Sirah	USA (CA)	$15
Conquista Shiraz	Argentina	$9
Cycles Gladiator Merlot	USA (CA)	$10
Cycles Gladiator Syrah	USA (CA)	$10
Dancing Bull Cabernet Sauvignon	USA (CA)	$12
Don Miguel Gascón Malbec	Argentina	$12

Heavy New World red *continued*

	Country	Price
Fairhills Malbec	Argentina	$10
Finca El Portillo Malbec	Argentina	$10
Fish Eye Cabernet Sauvignon	USA (CA)	$6
Gaucho Club Malbec	Argentina	$10
Geyser Peak Cabernet Sauvignon	USA (CA)	$15
Green Bridge Petite Sirah	USA (CA)	$8
Hahn Estates Cabernet Sauvignon	USA (CA)	$14
House Wine Red	USA (WA)	$12
Kaiken Cabernet Sauvignon	Argentina	$14
Liberty School Cabernet Sauvignon	USA (CA)	$15
Montes Malbec	Chile	$12
Norton Cabernet Sauvignon	Argentina	$11
Norton Malbec	Argentina	$11
Norton Merlot	Argentina	$11
Parducci Sustainable Red	USA (CA)	$10
Pascual Toso Malbec	Argentina	$13
Red Truck Petite Sirah	USA (CA)	$11
Rosemount Shiraz Diamond Label	Australia	$10
Round Hill Cabernet Sauvignon	USA (CA)	$8
Santa Julia Cabernet Sauvignon	Argentina	$11
337 Red	USA (CA)	$15
Trackers Crossing Cabernet Sauvignon	Australia	$8
Trapiche Malbec	Argentina	$9
Trapiche Cabernet Sauvignon	Argentina	$11
Vida Orgánica Malbec	Argentina	$9

Sweet or aromatic

	Country	Price
Château Ste. Michelle Riesling	USA (WA)	$10
Clean Slate Riesling	Germany	$11
Columbia Crest Two Vines Riesling	USA (WA)	$8
Conquista Torrontés	Argentina	$9
Fetzer Gewürztraminer	USA (CA)	$9
Ironstone "Obsession" Symphony	USA (CA)	$8
Kourtaki Mavrodaphne of Patras	Greece	$10
Norton Torrontés	Argentina	$11

2010 wine reviews

Alamos Malbec
Two-time Wine Trials selection

Style Heavy New World red
Country Argentina **Vintage tasted** 2008
Grapes Malbec
Drink with steak with creamed spinach
Website www.catenawines.com

Returning to the pages of *The Wine Trials*, this wine is the entry-level offering of the Argentine export industry's 800-pound gorilla. Catena's wines are much loved by the cheap-wine cognoscenti. This one is fruit-forward in the New World style and less subtle than some Malbecs, and it's a big, great-value wine to drink with an enormous hunk of meat.

Nose It's loaded with bright red fruit, although some blind tasters thought it smelled a bit cheap. Still, who doesn't like berries?

Mouth More red fruit here, along with a quality that one blind taster called "twigginess." The balance is impressive, with enough acid and tannin to keep the fruit from becoming cloying.

Design A dark, heavy, tapered bottle, minimalist writing, and a rugged Andes-scape create a rather imposing look, even if the contents are quite approachable.

Alice White Chardonnay
Two-time Wine Trials selection

Style Heavy New World white
Country Australia **Vintage tasted** 2008
Grapes Chardonnay
Drink with shellfish, risotto, white-sauce pasta dishes
Website www.alicewhite.com

We love to hate Australia's irritatingly popular "critter wine" producers, who often seem to spend more time drawing animal cartoons than making decent wine. Alice White's Chardonnay, however, is an exception to the rule—although this year's effort is less sprightly and more heavily oaked than the previous vintage, which won our "heavy New World whites" category last time. Still, honeyed flavors, decent acidity, and an exceptionally low price tag make this wine a superb value.

Nose Fans of oak will be pleased by the distinctly woody bouquet, but even the haters should enjoy the noticeable honey aromas.

Mouth The oak continues to dominate, but there's a slight prickle as well.

Design The marketing team plays off just about every Aussie stereotype, with the kangaroo roasting in the spirally sun. But the pleasantly austere sans-serif small-caps font beneath makes up for the clichés.

Almaden Chardonnay

Heritage • *Two-time Wine Trials Selection*

Style Light New World white
Country California   **Vintage tasted** Non-Vintage
Grapes Chardonnay
Drink with salmon, Brussels sprouts, cold pasta salads
Website www.almaden.com

Keep this box wine hidden under the table, and your guests might think you're serving them wine from a fairly expensive bottle. This wine isn't likely to blow you away—the flavors are pleasant but faint, and hardly distinctive—but at only a couple bucks for the equivalent of a bottle, we're still impressed. It's light, crisp, and easy drinking, closer to a French table wine than an oaky California monster. College students looking to offer something more drinkable than Franzia at their next dorm party, and even professionals hoping to serve a pleasant party wine that won't break the bank, should take note.

Nose There's a flowery, aromatic quality that our blind tasters had trouble pinpointing. If you take a deep whiff, you might pick up on tropical fruit as well.

Mouth It's round, but there's plenty of acid to provide balance.

Design If you're buying a box of wine, you're probably not that worried about the style factor. But you have to be amused by the green-and-gold insinuation that there's something royal about box wine.

Altano Douro

$8

Style Heavy Old World red
Country Portugal **Vintage tasted** 2006
Grapes Tinta Roriz, Touriga Franca
Drink with chorizo, Manchego cheese
Website www.symington.com

This wine hails from Portugal's Douro, the home of Port wine. It is made by Charles Symington, whose family is responsible for producing the great Ports of Graham's, Warre's, and Dow's. But while this wine is composed of Tinta Roriz and Touriga Franca, two of the grapes commonly used in Port, this red is definitely dry. It's a perfect table wine: it refuses to steal the stage or show off, but it will go well with a wide variety of foods.

Nose Strawberry and plum make appearances, but otherwise the nose isn't very impressive—one blind taster called it "the smell of neutrality."

Mouth There's plenty of red fruit here, with tannins and acidity to help it pair with food.

Design This bottle elevates the standard bottle clichés: the owl performs critter duty but at least doesn't look like a cartoon, while the red-and-black motif has given way to a more pleasing blue and orange.

Arancio Stemmari Nero d'Avola

$9

Sicilia IGT

Style Heavy Old World red
Country Italy **Vintage tasted** 2007
Grapes Nero d'Avola
Drink with grilled lamb chops, baked pasta
Website www.feudoarancio.it

Nero d'Avola is a Sicilian grape, and it shows: this wine is all about fiery spice and bold attitude. Like the Sicilians immortalized in films and novels, the wine is passionately welcoming—but you wouldn't want to get on its bad side. Originally used by unscrupulous vintners to beef up light reds throughout Europe, Nero d'Avola is finally being appreciated for the exciting, invigorating wine that it is. It's also food-friendly.

Nose Our blind tasters got a lot of aggressive berry and spice aromas.

Mouth It's extremely dense and concentrated—maybe a bit much by itself—but this makes the wine great with substantial foods.

Design The simple red-and-black bottle would be fine—if it weren't for the strange starfish creature that looks like it belongs on the walls of a child's bedroom. We recommend looking at the bottle from far away and just appreciating the colors.

Aveleda Fonte Vinho Verde

Two-time Wine Trials Selection

Style Light Old World white
Country Portugal **Vintage tasted** Non-Vintage
Grapes Trajadura, Loureiro, Arinto, Azal
Drink with sushi, gazpacho
Website www.aveleda.pt

$7

WINNER/BARGAIN

Not only is this Vinho Verde our Best of the Wine Trials winner in the light white category, but it clocks in at just seven bucks—making it the only bottle to capture both the Winner and Bargain crowns. The Fonte is crisp and lightly sparkling, in the classic Vinho Verde style. The ideal wine for cheap outdoor refreshment, it's meant to be drunk quickly: the word "verde" refers to the youthful greenness of the wine. We'll even admit to having drunk it over ice on the occasional hot summer day.

Nose There's plenty of orange, peach, and floral aromas here, with none of the sickliness that often accompanies light, aromatic wines at this price point.

Mouth The orange flavors continue, but it's impressively light and flowery. There's certainly some acid, but it's much less tart than your typical Vinho Verde.

Design It's busy but harmonious, with an appropriately green bottle and a nostalgic and colorful label.

Aveleda Quinta Vinho Verde

$9

Style Light Old World white
Country Portugal **Vintage tasted** 2008
Grapes Alvarinho, Loureiro, Trajadura
Drink with smoked herring, sushi
Website www.aveleda.pt

Aveleda is one of the big boys of Portuguese wine production, having graced tables across the spectrum—from college kids thrilled by the price tag to wine geeks excited by Vinho Verde. The "Quinta da Aveleda" version—a sort of cru Vinho Verde, if you will—only sets you back nine dollars; still, there are cheaper Vinhos Verdes out there, such as the Aveleda Fonte, which is this year's winner among light whites. And that one will only cost you seven dollars. Let's hear it for cheap wine.

Nose An intensely floral nose combines lavender and orange blossom—although the color is quite faint.

Mouth The prickle characteristic of Vinho Verde tipped some tasters off to its provenance. Still, they found continuing notes of florality and perfume, along with zippy acid.

Design We love the nostalgic yet simple sepia-toned label, especially against the light blue bottle. It's a class act—one of our favorites.

Barefoot Merlot
Two-time Wine Trials selection

Style Heavy New World red
Country California **Vintage tasted** Non-Vintage
Grapes Merlot
Drink with vegetable stews, roast turkey
Website www.barefootwine.com

Several Barefoot wines made it into this year's *Wine Trials*—although there are so many wines released each year by this producer that there are dozens of others on the market, too. This one, the only repeat winner among the Barefoots, is a bold, spicy, versatile Merlot that's big enough to push it into the "heavy" category. It's unmistakably cheap, but the strong flavors are enjoyable enough and will go well with a variety of foods and situations. For seven dollars, that's plenty impressive.

Nose Aggressive cherry aromas dominate, but there's also an ash-like smell that reminded one blind taster of a campfire.

Mouth Similar flavors in the mouth. As one taster said, it's decent but cheap.

Design Blue is definitely this foot's color. Otherwise, the design is simple and recognizable—at this price point, Barefoot is going for brand recognition, not style points.

Barefoot Pinot Grigio

$7 BARGAIN

Style Light New World white
Country California **Vintage tasted** Non-Vintage
Grapes Pinot Grigio
Drink with grilled fish, crab cakes
Website www.barefootwine.com

We have been happily surprised by several of the Barefoot wines, especially given their bargain-bin prices and ready availability. They're made in mass quantities, but they still retain a lot of character. This one, for instance, marries bright apple aromas with a crisp acidity that's a bit unusual in budget Pinot Grigios. We're grateful for the effort and relieved to know that we'll always be able to find one of these bottles in a pinch.

Nose Intense green apple dominates the other aromas—but hey, there are worse things out there.

Mouth The flavors are a bit more complex here, with oranges, flowers, and of course, more apple. There's also good acidity that one blind taster favorably characterized as "jumpy."

Design We like the foot motif, but yellow isn't its most flattering color. The bright shade also seems to clash with the color of the wine inside—all in all, not the best scheme.

Barefoot Zinfandel

Style Heavy New World red
Country California **Vintage tasted** Non-Vintage
Grapes Zinfandel
Drink with overstuffed sandwiches, chocolate cake
Website www.barefootwine.com

Normally a $7 Zin would have us running for the hills, but this one from Barefoot—a producer who has three bottles among our top-scoring wines—made us eat our words. And that's what blind tasting is all about: the moment when the brown bag is ripped off, and a room full of people realizes they were gushing over a wine sold at the corner gas station—although if you're feeling classier, you can probably find it at Trader Joe's, too.

Nose The first whiff might be of alcohol, but our more persistent blind tasters then smelled earthiness and tea leaves.

Mouth Structurally, the mouth holds together well, with decent tannins, jamminess, and spice.

Design A shiny metallic sticker, front and center, boasts of some second-rate wine award. On the other hand, wine medals are assigned almost randomly, according to professor Robert Hodgson—see pages 16–17 for more on his startling research.

Berço do Infante

$8

Style Heavy Old World red
Country Portugal **Vintage tasted** 2007
Grapes Castelão, Aragonez
Drink with blood sausage, charcuterie plate

While it doesn't have any spectacular superpowers, this is the type of wine that we are happy to recommend. It's an eminently affordable bottle from a totally underrepresented region: Portugal's remote Estremadura. None of our blind tasters was bowled over by the flavors here, but it's a perfectly fine wine for a casual dinner party. And at $8, that's not a bad proposition.

Nose Breathe deeply to really get the aromas, because otherwise they're quite faint. When you do get them, they're a bit nondescript, too—just a bit of fresh red fruit.

Mouth Multiple blind tasters described the taste as merely inoffensive, while plum was mentioned as a strong flavor.

Design This bottle is as understated, restrained, and inoffensive as its contents. It also carries an elegance in its simplicity.

Beringer Cabernet Sauvignon

Founders' Estate • *Two-time Wine Trials selection*

Style Heavy New World red
Country California **Vintage tasted** 2006
Grapes Cabernet Sauvignon
Drink with game birds, roast beef, lentil soup
Website www.beringer.com

The folks at Beringer really outdid themselves here…literally. In last year's *Wine Trials*, this $11 wine outscored their own $120 Beringer Private Reserve Cabernet. This year, our blind tasters were similarly enthusiastic about this eager-to-please wine. Big and peppery, it manages to maintain balance and will even go well with food. So hold on to your Benjamins, and pay for this wine with a Thomas. After all, Jefferson was a wine buff—Franklin was more of a beer guy.

Nose There's lots of red berries, black pepper, and a strong herbal note that reminded one blind taster of eucalyptus.

Mouth The same flavors continue, enhanced by impressive balance and food-friendly tannins.

Design Misguided. The strange swoop on the right side of the label just ends up looking like a mistake. But for $109 in savings, we can handle an ugly bottle.

Black Box Cabernet Sauvignon
Two-time Wine Trials selection

Style Heavy New World red
Country California **Vintage tasted** 2007
Grapes Cabernet Sauvignon
Drink with meatloaf, pot roast
Website www.blackboxwines.com

Put your snobbery aside: Box wine has many advantages, including larger volume and lower production costs, and vacuum-sealed bags mean that you can keep the wine open for days or even weeks without significant loss of flavor. Still, we can't quite imagine keeping a big box of wine on the table for our next dinner party. We're working on it—people say that box wines are the next big thing in the industry, so we'll have to adjust. And as this simple, fairly elegant Cabernet shows, good wines can come in square packages.

Nose Our blind tasters enjoyed the red berry and plum aromas, along with a hint of pepper.

Mouth It's impressively balanced, with decent acidity and firm tannins. It would make a great food wine—if you have the guts to serve it at dinner.

Design Well, it's a black box, so we have to give it credit for following through on its name. Otherwise, with the cheesy gold font and purple graphic, it won't be winning many style awards.

Block No. 45 Petite Sirah

$7

BARGAIN

Style Heavy New World red
Country California **Vintage tasted** 2007
Grapes Petite Sirah
Drink with steak, beef stew

Misleading name aside, Petite Sirah is not a milder version of Syrah: in fact, they are two distinct grapes, and Petite Sirah is much bolder, more tannic, fruitier, and all-around bigger than its namesake. Block No. 45's version is no exception. It's big, juicy, and tannic—a perfect choice for a steak on a cold winter evening.

Nose It's big and jammy, with plenty of berries and plums. Some of our tasters thought it was a bit too big, in fact.

Mouth The mouth follows through on the promise of the nose: huge and spicy, it's got loads of tannins.

Design We loved this design. Bold fonts, a strong color scheme, and rectangles arranged like an Abstract Expressionist piece give this wine an elegant, avant-garde feel. It came close to going over the top with the faux-degraded typewriter font...but, in the end, remained just beneath the top.

Bogle Cabernet Sauvignon

Style Heavy New World red
Country California **Vintage tasted** 2007
Grapes Cabernet Sauvignon
Drink with rabbit stew, gumbo
Website www.boglewinery.com

Though not the favorite of the Bogles blind tasted this year, the Cabernet Sauvignon is one of an impressive three wines from this producer to make it into *The Wine Trials 2010*. Interestingly, no white wines from Bogle won favor from blind tasters this year (the Sauvignon Blanc was previously a darling). Bogle seems to have done better this year with the big, expansive flavors of their reds.

Nose Based on the aromas, many blind tasters incorrectly pegged this as a Shiraz; they found notes of eucalyptus, a common trait of that grape. One taster remarked that the aromas were sophisticated.

Mouth Very well developed and tannic. This wine could even age a bit more before you drink it.

Design These Bogle bottles are hefty, and their weight is a nice feature—one that often tricks people into thinking the wine is more expensive than it really is. The distressed look of the label adds a classy touch, too.

Bogle Old Vine Zinfandel

Two-time Wine Trials selection

$11

Style Heavy New World red
Country California **Vintage tasted** 2007
Grapes Zinfandel
Drink with pulled pork, game meats
Website www.boglewinery.com

Zinfandel is a pretty divisive grape; its manifestations are often concentrated, in-your-face, and to some people, just too sweet. But if Zinfandel is your thing, the Bogle is a totally honest version (both in this vintage and last year's). It's a classic New World expression of the grape, with highly concentrated fruit, a touch of sweetness, and plenty of oak. And at 14.8% alcohol, this vintage is even more alcoholic than the last. Proceed with caution.

Nose Big, juicy aromas of blackberry, plum, and tea leaves jump out of the glass.

Mouth It's a little on the sweet side, but there's a murky mix of dark, spicy fruit to counterbalance.

Design The subtly tapered Bogle bottle is a model of power and elegance. The creeping, almost primeval vine graphic and deep black background seem to echo the wine's qualities. This is one of our favorite bottles in the book.

Bogle Pinot Noir

Style Light New World red
Country California **Vintage tasted** 2007
Grapes Pinot Noir
Drink with Thanksgiving turkey, sausage
Website www.boglewinery.com

This little Pinot packs a big punch. Our blind tasters loved the complexity and exotic aromas, especially in a wine in this price range. With three wines in this year's *Wine Trials* and two in last year's, Bogle definitely deserves a pat on the back. Let's just hope that they can continue to turn out wines with this much value.

Nose It has great berry aromas, but not everyone is a fan of the earthy scents one taster likened to vinyl and rubber.

Mouth There's more cherry here, with a complex herbal flavor as well.

Design The signature Bogle label doesn't look too bad on this well crafted bottle, but it still isn't our favorite.

Bonterra Chardonnay

Style Heavy New World white
Country California **Vintage tasted** 2007
Grapes Chardonnay
Drink with creamy potato soup, curry dishes
Website www.bonterra.com

Bonterra's grapes are "grown organically," but the wine is not "certified organic." This comes to the heart of a controversy in the wine world: to get organic certification, producers must ditch sulfites, which can have disastrous consequences for their wine. Environmentally sustainable practices are much more important, so we applaud its producer for the growing methods—and for making this delicious, easy-to-enjoy Chard.

Nose There's a definite butteriness and even what one blind taster identified as bread. But there's also apple and perky citrus.

Mouth Bracing acidity, a bit of honey, and apple. It all ends in a mouthwatering finish.

Design It's very early-'90s California. If Bonterra is going to engage in progressive viticulture, they could also engage in progressive design. But if they're going to pick a side, focusing on what's inside the bottle is the right one.

Bus Stop Red

$10

Fairhills

Style Heavy New World red
Country Argentina **Vintage tasted** 2007
Grapes Bonarda, Shiraz, Merlot
Drink with grass-fed, sustainable organic beef, compassion

Next time you think to yourself, "Wow, I'd love a $10 bottle of wine right now, but I should really use that money to help educate third-world workers," don't worry: proceeds from this fair trade, do-gooder wine help pay for education in the Argentine communities surrounding the winery. On a more selfish note, the wine is quite nice, with bright flavors that reminded our blind tasters of a Beaujolais.

Nose It's got ripe cherry aromas, along with a hint of bell pepper. Some of our blind tasters weren't big fans—one was reminded of the smell of methane.

Mouth There's a green, astringent quality that balances the bright berry flavors.

Design It may be noble, but it isn't pretty. The silver motif clashes with the wavy reds and oranges, and it seems a bit tacky to brag about its environmental stewardship right on the front of the bottle.

Cabriz

Quinta de Cabriz, Dão Sul

$11

Style Heavy Old World red
Country Portugal **Vintage tasted** 2006
Grapes Alfrocheiro, Tinta Roriz, Touriga Nacional
Drink with duck breast, French onion soup
Website www.daosul.com

The Dão region of Portugal is often said to be that country's Burgundy. The wines are made mostly by small farmers rather than huge corporations, and the style is usually restrained, elegant, and distinctly food-friendly...right up our alley. This effort from Dão Sul is jammier and more concentrated than most Dão wines, but it's still impressively balanced and earthy. It should pair well with everything from steak to grilled chicken.

Nose Our blind tasters identified sour cherry, earth, and barnyard aromas—we can understand the comparison to Burgundy.

Mouth It's sleek and spicy. There's jam here, but it adds to the balance rather than overwhelming it.

Design This strangely proportioned Burgundy-ish bottle is a little homely. The drawing of the church seems like it was done by a decently talented child; we're not quite sure what they're going for. The raised glass on is a nice touch, though.

Caldora Montepulciano d'Abruzzo

$11

D.O.C.

Style Light Old World red
Country Italy **Vintage tasted** 2008
Grapes Montepulciano
Drink with pork loin, duck ragù

Montepulciano can be a tricky word for those first trying Italian wines. There is Vino Nobile di Montepulciano, where Montepulciano refers to the town of origin (these wines are made from Sangiovese grapes). And then there's Montepulciano d'Abruzzo, where Montepulciano is the name of the grape from which the wine is made. Lusher and less acidic than many Italian wines, Montepulciano d'Abruzzo is a great way for New World drinkers to explore Italian wine without suffering from culture shock.

Nose It's packed with deep, black fruit—one blind taster identified it as cassis.

Mouth Again, rich fruit predominates, along with a hint of vanilla.

Design We like the minimalism and intense simplicity of the bottle. We were a bit puzzled by the diamond shape cut out of the label, though—maybe they're cutting paper costs?

Campo Viejo Rioja Crianza
Two-time Wine Trials selection

Style Light Old World red
Country Spain **Vintage tasted** 2006
Grapes Tempranillo, Garnacha, Mazuelo
Drink with roast duck, lamb, robust cheeses
Website www.campoviejo.com

This wine reminds us of what wine used to taste like before the emergence of the in-your-face "international" style. It's earthy, aromatic, floral, and as one blind taster said, understated; after sampling dozens of ostentatious California Cabernets, our blind tasters found that subtlety to be a definite virtue. Crianza is aged longer than most inexpensive wines, so it's mature, too—and complex. Some argue that Rioja needs to be drunk with food, but we'd drink this one anytime, anyplace.

Nose It's delicate and aromatic, with floral aromas and vanilla. One blind taster was even reminded of cookies.

Mouth Big and fruity at first, it fades into beautiful flavors our tasters compared to smoke and leather before resolving into soft tannins.

Design You won't impress anyone with this bottle. The font cheesily evokes Old Europe, although at least the bright yellow label is eye-catching.

Campo Viejo Rioja Reserva

$13

Style Light Old World red
Country Spain **Vintage tasted** 2004
Grapes Tempranillo, Graciano, Mazuelo
Drink with chorizo, lamb chops
Website www.campoviejo.com

The flavors of this Reserva are complex and unusual, and it has the kind of balance and food-friendly acidity for which Rioja is known. The winemakers at Campo Viejo have clearly resisted the trend for syrupy fruit bombs; instead, they produce wines that are subtle and idiosyncratic. We recommend that anyone who's never had a distinctly Old World wine try it—the flavors may not sound like something you'd want to taste, but we think you'll enjoy the experience.

Nose Our blind tasters identified everything from red fruit to vegetal and barnyard aromas to motor oil.

Mouth It's spicy and substantial, with dark cherry, herbs, and a hint of barnyard flavors. There's also a nice acid kick to give the wine structure.

Design The label color is richer than the Crianza's, presumably to reflect the extra aging and complexity of the wine. We're still not huge fans of the cheesy font, though.

Casa Silva Carménère Reserve

$13

Style Light New World red
Country Chile **Vintage tasted** 2006
Grapes Carménère
Drink with churrasco
Website www.casasilva.cl

Carménère used to be of one of the mysteries of the wine world. Throughout the twentieth century, drinkers were puzzled as to why Chilean Merlot was so distinctively different from French, American, or even Argentine Merlot. It was only in 1994 that a professor of oenology discovered that many supposed Chilean Merlot vines were, in fact, Carménère, a little-planted Bordeaux grape variety. Although other nations have since discovered Carménère vines within their borders, it is Chile that has become known for great Carménère wines, which are usually rich, supple, and excellent values.

Nose It's smoky and peppery, and aggressive enough that one blind taster called it stinky.

Mouth The balance is impressive, and there are flavors of cocoa and cola—all in all, a real crowd-pleaser.

Design Something about the odd layout, gold seal, and strange text colors makes us anxious. It's definitely a miss.

Casal Garcia Vinho Verde

Two-time Wine Trials selection

Style Light Old World white
Country Portugal **Vintage tasted** Non-Vintage
Grapes Pedernã, Loureiro, Trajadura, Azal
Drink with sushi, ceviche, carpaccio, raw oysters
Website www.casalgarcia.com

Appearing for the second time in *The Wine Trials*, Casal Garcia's refreshing offering contributes to the strong Vinho Verde showing in this year's edition. A bright, effervescent, summery wine, this bottle should be served at a colder temperature than non-sparkling whites. While Vinho Verde is technically not considered sparkling, there is a slight carbon-dioxide prickle. This allows it to pair easily with many different fresh, cold foods—a trick that sommeliers love to use. This could be the sushi wine to end all.

Nose Our blind tasters identified spice and bubble gum, although some complained that the nose was a bit faint.

Mouth It's light, tart, and refreshing, with the slight effervescent prickle common to Vinho Verde.

Design The lace background and coat of arms are far too frilly, but the designers avoid the great-aunt's-house look through decent symmetry and harmony.

Casteller Cava

$13

FINALIST

Style Sparkling
Country Spain **Vintage tasted** Non-Vintage
Grapes Xarel-lo, Macabeo, Parellada
Drink with pear and walnut salad, lightly seared fish

Cava, Spain's most famous bubbly, is the hot new thing in the world of sparkling wine. It's usually sharp and clean, with none of the yeasty or creamy flavors that define a good Champagne. That refreshing quality, along with impressive value, makes Cava the ideal summer bubbly for sipping on the porch with friends. Casteller produces a Cava that's richer and creamier than most—a good transition wine for Champagne drinkers looking to find a sparkling wine they can drink without an excuse.

Nose It's toasty and full, with aromas of green apple.

Mouth Bright, refreshing acidity makes for a clean feel in the mouth. The apple flavors linger longer than you would expect—our blind tasters were enthusiastic.

Design The lone castle—Casteller is a Catalan word meaning castle-builder—is a model of simplicity and restraint. It does look a bit ominous, though.

Castello di Querceto Chianti

DOCG

$10

Style Light Old World red
Country Italy **Vintage tasted** 2007
Grapes Sangiovese, Trebbiano, Colorino, Malvasia
Drink with game meats, roast chicken
Website www.castellodiquerceto.it

Chianti went through an unfortunate period in the '70s when the wicker baskets that housed the wine were given more attention than the liquid itself; quality dropped off and Chianti became known as Italian for "undrinkable." Indeed, many older drinkers still think of Chianti as cheap plonk. Thankfully, the Tuscan winemakers got their acts together, and Chiantis are now generally well-made and delicious. One taster described this one as having a light and fruity nose with a dark and spicy mouth: sounds like it's got all its bases covered.

Nose The earthy aromas are distinctly Old World, but there's enough fruit to satisfy even the most ardent New World fan.

Mouth It's dark and rich, but still simple and easy to drink.

Design The rich blue color, simple font, textured paper, and elegant graphic together suggest cheesiness...but also costliness.

Castello Monaci Pilùna
Salento IGT

Style Heavy Old World red
Country Italy **Vintage tasted** 2007
Grapes Primitivo
Drink with hamburgers, short ribs
Website www.castellomonaci.it

This wine hails from Puglia, the heel of Italy's boot. It's made of Primitivo—(arguably) known in the United States as Zinfandel—and like good American Zins, these wines are often concentrated and powerful. But the Italian influence inevitably shows up, and most Primitivo offerings are more restrained and a bit more elegant than their American cousins. This one, which tasters liked enough to send to the finals, is even more Old World in style than most, with a woodiness and spice that's distinctly European. Primitivo is definitely an "in" grape right now.

Nose It's spicy, with a mulchy smell that's definitely Italian.

Mouth It has a careful balance, with soft, smooth tannins. The flavors are a bit tight at first, but give them a moment and they'll open up.

Design Impressively elegant. No critters or château sketches here— just an off-white label cut in half, with well-chosen fonts and a simple color scheme. Excellent work.

Cave de Lugny Mâcon-Villages

$11

Two-time Wine Trials selection

Style Heavy Old World white
Country France **Vintage tasted** 2007
Grapes Chardonnay
Drink with lobster, grilled shrimp, pasta salad
Website www.cave-lugny.com

Drinkers who have sworn off Chardonnay because of its typically heavy, over-oaked style and seeming incompatibility with food ought to take another look at white Burgundy wines. These wines are what first made the Chardonnay grape's reputation, and they can reach stunning heights of quality—and, unfortunately, of price, too. Happily, the local village wines in Burgundy can be great values for those looking for a break from the California style: instead of rich, buttery texture and huge body, the wines produced by Cave de Lugny and its peers are clean, crisp, packed with minerality, and tingling with acidity.

Nose Minerals, minerals, minerals. Think wet rocks or exposed slate.

Mouth It has exciting balance, with sharp acidity and continuing minerality.

Design It's a pretty run-of-the-mill white Burgundy bottle, outdated and vaguely evocative of a stuffy banquet in an awkward ballroom.

Charamba Douro

Style Light Old World red
Country Portugal **Vintage tasted** 2005
Grapes Touriga Nacional, Touriga Francesa, Tinta Barroca
Drink with Mexican food, feijoada, cassoulet
Website www.aveleda.pt

Portugal is one of the best countries in the world for wine value, and this spicy, exciting bottle is no exception to that rule. Produced by Aveleda—also responsible for one of the year's best Vinho Verdes—this wine is made up of many of the same grape varieties that compose Port. Rather than being sweet, though, this wine is dry and tannic, with a peppery spiciness that reminds us of some of our favorite Rhône wines. Why can't every red at this price point be as tasty and interesting?

Nose It's intensely spicy: our blind tasters identified black pepper, all-spice, cayenne, and fresh peppercorns.

Mouth It's got a nice earthiness, along with healthy doses of acidity and tannin. It should pair beautifully with stewed red meat.

Design The font is silly safari-chic, and the wavy lines evoke hills. This label is not among our favorites, to say the least, even though the wine inside most definitely is.

Charles Shaw Cabernet Sauvignon

"Two-Buck Chuck" • *Two-time Wine Trials selection*

Style Heavy New World red
Country California **Vintage tasted** 2007
Grapes Cabernet Sauvignon
Drink with recently delivered pizza

It's ba-ack! Two-Buck Chuck, beloved by college students and contrarian penny pinchers, has once again made the cut to be among the top 150 wines in this year's blind tastings—not because it's great, but because value counts. The same syrupy quality was present in this year's vintage, and we still maintain that this just might be what Houston rap stars are referencing when they talk about "sizzurp." Skip the sizzurp, and sip the Shaw.

Nose It's nothing too complex, but simple fruit aromas are most definitely there.

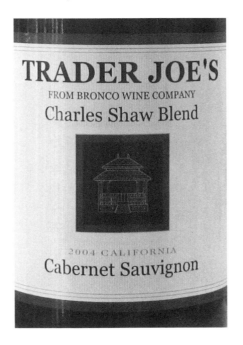

Mouth There's not too much varietal character present, but blind tasters noted juicy red fruit and a slightly chemical taste to the wine.

Design Don't look for the words "Two-Buck Chuck" anywhere on the rote, poorly designed label (that straight quote is downright offensive); just call him Charles Shaw.

Charles Shaw Chardonnay

"Two-Buck Chuck" • *Two-time Wine Trials selection*

Style Heavy New World white
Country California **Vintage tasted** 2007
Grapes Chardonnay
Drink with fish and chips, or just chips

Yes, it's Two-Buck Chuck, and its reputation will always precede it. (It actually costs three bucks in most of the country.) You've probably tried the Chuck at some point—even if just out of curiosity—but our blind tasters were once again surprised this year to find that they actually liked this cheapest of cheap wines. Take our recommendation under advisement, however: the Two-Buck Chuck often differs in quality from one batch to the next.

Nose Very faint oak and toast were most noticeable.

Mouth It was easy for blind tasters to correctly identify this as a California Chardonnay, even if some complained that it was one-dimensional.

Design A seventh-grader with default Windows fonts and Microsoft Word could probably produce something better. At least there's no outline text. Or flashing screen font, like on the old Commodore 128.

Château Bonnet Red

$15

Style Light Old World red
Country France **Vintage tasted** 2005
Grapes Cabernet Sauvignon, Merlot
Drink with grilled vegetables, skirt steak
Website www.andrelurton.com

There's a reason France remains synonymous with great wine in the minds of many drinkers: the country produces wines that range from the sublime to the easy-drinking but are always distinctly French. Château Bonnet is a simple bistro wine, but it's packed with the earthiness that screams French terroir. It proves that great values exist even in Bordeaux, which is a lesson we're always happy to learn.

Nose It's a bit faint, but our blind tasters liked the earthy aromas of mineral and mulch that accompany the red fruit.

Mouth Some felt it was a bit thin, but there's still plenty here to pair with simple bistro food; it will show best with a meal. You might expect a Bordeaux blend to be in the "heavy" category. Not this one.

Design Simple fonts, white background, small sketch of an elegant château—they're clearly following a formula. Still, it's a good formula, so who are we to complain?

Château Bonnet White

$13

Style Light Old World white
Country France **Vintage tasted** 2008
Grapes Sauvignon Blanc, Sémillon, Muscadelle
Drink with seared tuna, roast chicken
Website www.andrelurton.com

The red wines of Bordeaux get all the glory, but white Bordeaux wines can be delicious and even profound in their own right: the Sauvignon Blanc grape provides racy acidity and intense aromas, while softer Sémillon provides body and subtlety. This excellent bottle, one of two Château Bonnet wines in this year's *Wine Trials*, combines tight acidity and complex flavors without breaking the bank. While it would be delicious as an apéritif, it will really shine as a food wine, complementing anything from seafood to turkey.

Nose The complex aromas include orange and lime. The nose is restrained, though, and some tasters thought it was somewhat faint.

Mouth Beautiful citrus flavors dominate. It's noticeably tart.

Design The green rectangle adds some life to what is otherwise a staid label. It's nothing special, but at least it doesn't actively detract from the wine.

Château Ste. Michelle Pinot Gris

Columbia Valley • *Two-time Wine Trials selection*

Style Light New World white
Country Washington State **Vintage tasted** 2008
Grapes Pinot Gris, Viognier
Drink with crawfish, grilled shrimp, crab cakes
Website www.ste-michelle.com

Château Ste. Michelle produces great Alsace-style wines with a Washington State twist. For the second year in a row, this Pinot Gris is among their best efforts. It's got more character than most Italian Pinot Grigios, plus zippy acidity and a nice crisp mouthfeel—so crisp that some found it to be almost prickly. It's a refreshing wine, especially on a hot day, or with a heaping plate of shellfish. There's only one thing that irks us: why can't there be more wines like this coming out of the United States?

Nose There's a distinct lemon-lime aroma that's pleasant if unexciting.

Mouth This is where the wine really shines. It's steely and tart, with citrus, orange, and banana flavors.

Design The papery label is elegant, and the slight lifted section along the top is an interesting touch. Let's work on the froofy cursive, though.

Château Ste. Michelle Riesling

Columbia Valley • *Two-time Wine Trials selection*

Style Aromatic New World white
Country Washington State **Vintage tasted** 2008
Grapes Riesling
Drink with Thai curries, lamb vindaloo, jerk chicken
Website www.ste-michelle.com

Château Ste. Michelle makes one of the few American Rieslings that we can wholeheartedly recommend. You'll definitely want to drink this one with food, though. It's not sweet enough to stand on its own as a dessert wine, yet it's too sweet to stand and sip at a bar. You'd do best to pair it with spicy dishes that would ordinarily overwhelm something less flowery. We think a dry Austrian or Alsatian Riesling would be worth the extra few bucks; still, many of our blind tasters loved this wine.

Nose It's aromatic and flowery, with a component that some blind tasters found almost nutty.

Mouth There's plenty of bright acid to complement the sweetness and florality, but we think they could have dialed it up even more.

Design The label's pompous script reminds us of a stuffy hotel restaurant. And this is clearly a case of Anglicization gone too far: the circumflex accent is missing in the word "Château."

Château Ste. Michelle Sauvignon Blanc $9

Columbia Valley • *Two-time Wine Trials selection*

Style Light New World white
Country Washington State **Vintage tasted** 2008
Grapes Sauvignon Blanc
Drink with goat cheese salad, ceviche
Website www.ste-michelle.com

Now *this* is a Sauvignon Blanc. It's not as in-your-face as some of what you see coming out of New Zealand, and for that we like it. The style is a nice blend of Old World and New: the region's cool climate ensures that grapes aren't overripe or the wines too sweet. Château Ste. Michelle has consistently fared well with *Wine Trials* blind tasters and with the wine world at large; they seem to have mastered the art of producing delicious, interesting wines for the budget drinker.

Nose It has plenty of fresh apple and floral aromas, though some blind tasters found it a bit chemical.

Mouth Our blind tasters loved the slight prickle on the palate. And while it may not be as blisteringly tart as a New Zealand Sauv Blanc, there's plenty of crisp acidity to go around.

Design It's got that classic Château Ste. Michelle look: trying to be classy, but ending up old and stilted, largely because of the cursive font.

CK Mondavi Chardonnay

Style Heavy New World white
Country California **Vintage tasted** 2008
Grapes Chardonnay
Drink with chilled vegetable soup, creamy pastas
Website www.ckmondavi.com

Don't call it Robert Mondavi. The "CK" stands for Charles Krug, which is the winery on the other side of the family—Peter Mondavi's side. Yes, these wines are completely mass produced, but they're often strikingly drinkable for the price point. This Chardonnay wine has the fruit, restrained oak, and balanced acidity that we look for. And at the price of a New York beer, that's pretty impressive.

Nose There's a bit more oak than we'd like, and a distinct aroma of butter comes along with it. There's also fruit here, with tasters finding pineapple and papaya.

Mouth The tropical fruit continues, but it's matched by healthy acidity and a slight metallic edge, and the oak falls off enough not to dominate.

Design We're never huge fans of winery crests on budget bottles, and the many different fonts are overwhelming. This is bad design, pure and simple.

Clean Slate Riesling
Mosel

Style Aromatic Old World white
Country Germany **Vintage tasted** 2007
Grapes Riesling
Drink with pork tenderloin, smoked salmon
Website www.cleanslatewine.com

Dollar for dollar, it's hard to beat a good German Riesling. Weightless but intense, sweet but bitingly acidic, aromatic but grounded, German Riesling defies easy categorization. For a value bottle, this wine has excellent pedigree: "Clean Slate" references the rocky flavor for which the Mosel, one of the best viticultural areas in Germany, is known. And as luck would have it, this wine is from 2007, a vintage widely thought to be one of the best in a decade, if not longer. Our blind tasters liked it enough to send it to the finals, where it won Best of the Wine Trials in the sweet and aromatic category.

Nose It's a classic German nose with loads of minerality—including, we assume, slate. Good stuff.

Mouth There's some nice fruit here, but the star attraction is the exciting give and take between the sugar and the acidity.

Design It's sleek yet pointed, just like the wine. We love the narrow label and clean fonts.

Columbia Crest Two Vines Riesling ($8)

Style Aromatic New World white
Country Washington State **Vintage tasted** 2007
Grapes Riesling
Drink with oysters, aged cheese (not together)
Website www.columbiacrest.com

Unlike many New World Rieslings, which can be insipid or cloying, this wine is light, refreshing, and just plain fun to drink. Like any good Riesling, it walks a delicate tightrope between sweetness and acidity. We'll happily drink this bottle outdoors on a hot summer day, or as a complement to shellfish.

Nose The aromatic nose of peaches, apricots, and minerals was a hit with our tasters. There's even a hint of the gasoline-ish scent often associated (but not in a bad way) with older Riesling.

Mouth Sugar, fruit, minerality, acidity—just what we want in an inexpensive Riesling.

Design Compared to the other labels in the Columbia Crest portfolio, this design is a work of art. The sleek bottle, elegant glass, and well-chosen color scheme showcase the wine perfectly.

Columbia Crest Two Vines Shiraz

$8

Style Heavy New World red
Country Washington State **Vintage tasted** 2005
Grapes Shiraz
Drink with steak, lamb chops
Website www.columbiacrest.com

Columbia Crest is Washington State's mass-market powerhouse, with a portfolio that includes four different lines of wines, of which Two Vines is the lowest priced. Our blind tasters tried several of the wines from the more expensive Grand Estates line, and rejected them all as overbearing. This Shiraz, on the other hand, might benefit from being in the budget line: rather than being a huge fruit bomb with loads of raspberry jam, it's smoky, meaty, and a little vegetal. Our blind tasters were intrigued, and we were too—it's hard not to support an inexpensive Shiraz that actually shows a little character.

Nose It's got cherry, smoke, and a vegetal aroma that reminded one blind taster of bell pepper.

Mouth It's a nice blend of red berries, plums, meat, and some food-friendly acid.

Design The new Two Vines labels are elegant in their simplicity, although the blue-and-gold color scheme on this particular bottle feels outdated.

Concannon Petite Sirah

Limited Release • *Two-time Wine Trials selection*

Style Heavy New World red
Country California **Vintage tasted** 2006
Grapes Petite Sirah
Drink with oven-roasted chicken, beef tenderloin
Website www.concannonvineyard.com

Concannon built its reputation on Petite Sirah, and the folks there claim to have produced the world's first single-varietal version. Their skill at turning out a dense, luscious Petite Sirah—with flavors and aromas that wouldn't be out of place in a $30 or $40 bottle of wine—certainly bolsters their claim. If you're a fan of bold, powerful New World reds that aren't sweet or jammy, this bottle, which came close to making the finals, should hit the spot.

Nose Rich black fruit and dark chocolate dominate, with subtle hints of toffee and coffee underneath. As one blind taster said, it smells expensive.

Mouth More dark fruit and chocolate here. The tannins can be aggressive at first.

Design We find the raised graphic fascinating. While the bottom of the tree is tight and controlled, the branches transform into a semi-abstract splatter straight out of Jackson Pollock's portfolio.

Concannon Pinot Noir
Limited Release

Style Light New World red
Country California **Vintage tasted** 2007
Grapes Pinot Noir
Drink with duck, green salad with pancetta
Website www.concannonvineyard.com

We're always pleasantly surprised to find a cheap New World Pinot that has more to it than ripe cherries. This one tastes almost Burgundian, with a salty, earthy profile and complex flavors. It's exciting to find a good Pinot like this one, because you can be confident it will pair with a huge variety of food. Whether it's duck confit, a roast chicken, or even a heavily sauced salmon, this wine will stand up quite well—as it did in the finals, where it missed the Best of the Wine Trials award by only a hair (edged out by the LAN Rioja) in the light red wine category.

Nose It's wonderfully earthy; there's cherry here, but a rich, mulchy aroma dominates.

Mouth There's more cherry, along with a lively, spicy quality that our blind tasters adored.

Design Very impressive. The raised paper design complements nicely the raised glass, and the designers aren't afraid to let the white space speak for itself.

Conquista Shiraz

$9

Style Heavy New World red
Country Argentina **Vintage tasted** 2007
Grapes Shiraz
Drink with lean cuts of beef, lamb chops

Drinkers in search of the massive oak-and-fruit cocktail that is a typical Australian Shiraz will be disappointed by this bottle: while there's plenty of ripe fruit, the overall profile of this Argentine wine is closer to Old World restraint than New World bombast. Which is why we like it. And which is why we wish it had been marketed under the more elegant name of Syrah. (Syrah and Shiraz are the French and Australian names for the same grape.) But we suppose you can't underestimate consumer loyalty to the Down Under spelling.

Nose There's plenty of fruit, but also a mulchy, earthy, fertilizer-like smell that's rich and enjoyable.

Mouth It's a well-balanced Old-World-style food wine, with strong green flavors.

Design This is an interesting design idea, and we like the framed graphics side by side. We're not huge fans of the bright, busy pattern running up the neck of the bottle, though.

Conquista Torrontés

$9
FINALIST

Style Aromatic New World white
Country Argentina **Vintage tasted** 2008
Grapes Torrontés
Drink with Tex-Mex, rich risotto

Naming a wine after the European conquistadors who first subjugated the territory that would become Argentina seems politically incorrect—but who are we to judge? This wine is made from Torrontés, the characteristic white grape of Argentina. A good Torrontés, like this one, can be wonderfully floral, aromatic, and clean. With the rising popularity of Argentine Malbec, it's about time that Argentina's whites begin to get the recognition they deserve.

Nose The lush nose is packed with aromas of orange, honey, tropical fruit, and rose. Blind tasters were impressed with the intensity and variety of the smells.

Mouth It has a long, tight finish that was a hit with our tasters.

Design We still like the Conquista label design, but the colors are less striking against the pale wine that shows through the bottle. Their reds definitely look prettier.

Cortijo Rioja

$10

Style Light Old World red
Country Spain **Vintage tasted** 2008
Grapes Tempranillo, Garnacha
Drink with lamb tagine, pork chop
Website www.aldeanueva.com

For at least the past decade, there has been a small civil war raging in Rioja between the traditionalists, who favor time-tested winemaking methods and an Old World style, and the modernists, who prefer fruit-forward, "international" flavors. Unlike many of the other winning Riojas in this year's blind tastings, this wine is firmly in the modernist camp. It's big and jammy, with so much fruit that it can seem almost sweet. But in a nod to tradition, the wine includes flavors of pepper and mint typical in old-style Rioja.

Nose It's fruit-forward and jammy, with noticeable alcohol that reminded one blind taster of vinyl.

Mouth There's more red fruit here, along with dark chocolate, floral flavors, a huge body, and a taste that one blind taster identified as tobacco leaf.

Design Simple and understated, the design is Spanish-hip, right down to the childish rendering of a house.

Crane Lake Chardonnay
California

$7

Style Heavy New World white
Country California **Vintage tasted** 2008
Grapes Chardonnay, French Colombard
Drink with crab cakes, jerk chicken
Website www.cranelakewines.com

Stuffed with interesting scents and flavors, this well-balanced, slightly off-dry wine is everything an inexpensive California Chardonnay should be, plus some extra residual sugar. Although its strong oak and vanilla flavors mark it as distinctly modern Californian, the wine manages to present refreshing acidity and subtle fruit flavors. If only more Chardonnay producers would take the hint.

Nose A mix of vanilla, Granny Smith apple, mineral, and pear. More exotically, one taster was reminded of the inside of an empty SweeTarts box.

Mouth Flavors of vanilla, spice, apples, honey, and lime dominate the palate, but decent acidity keeps the wine from seeming cloying.

Design The label is as neat and unpretentious as the wine. Everything, from the dignified crane, to the restrained parchment effect, to the simple font, says class without pomposity. And doesn't say $7.

Crane Lake Pinot Grigio
California

Style Light New World white
Country California **Vintage tasted** 2008
Grapes Pinot Grigio, Chardonnay, French Colombard
Drink with cheese and crackers on a hot summer day
Website www.cranelakewines.com

This winery's name sounds suspiciously like a housing development, and our research has discovered no Crane Lake in California. Cryptic name aside, this fruity little number delivers everything you could ask for in a cheap Pinot Grigio: plenty of fruit, refreshing citrus, minerality, and...drumroll please...sugar. Still, it's decent for a pre-dinner drink on the porch with friends.

Nose Our tasters detected flowers, tropical fruit, citrus, and yes, just a hint of pee. Don't worry, that's a compliment.

Mouth Plenty of citrus and white peach flavors. A healthy dose of acidity helps this Pinot Grigio stay very well balanced.

Design While they may have latched onto the trend for so-called "critter wines," the label is pleasantly simple and understated—the designers managed to resist the urge to make the crane juggle or ride a bicycle.

Cycles Gladiator Merlot

California

$10

Style Heavy New World red
Country California **Vintage tasted** 2007
Grapes Merlot, Cabernet Sauvignon
Drink with risotto, sausage
Website www.cyclesgladiator.com

There aren't many wines that can say they've been banned in the state of Alabama. After Cycles' label was deemed pornographic in the state, the winery did the only logical thing it could: it sold tee shirts. The shirts, which featured a crossed-out copy of the label and the catchy tag line "taste what they're missing," are surprisingly stylish. We might order a few as collector's items.

Nose There's a distinct aroma of cola—one blind taster specified that it was Cherry Coke—as well as red berries and green pepper. There's also a noticeable chemical edge to the nose.

Mouth Even though there's Merlot than Cab in this blend, this wine tastes remarkably like the latter, with green vegetal aromas and healthy tannins.

Design Original prints of this evocative 19th-century French bicycle-ad drawing go for as much as $50,000. We wouldn't pay that much, but we do love the artwork.

Cycles Gladiator Syrah

$10

Central Coast

Style Heavy New World red
Country California **Vintage tasted** 2007
Grapes Syrah, Petite Sirah
Drink with lamb tagine, Irish stew
Website www.cyclesgladiator.com

This wine has a bit of an identity crisis; on the nose there are whispers of an Australian Shiraz, but there isn't the aggressive, burnt-rubber mouth that we fear in that genre. The mouth is more California in its somewhat-reined-in fruitiness. Meanwhile, the label is wishing it were French.

Nose It's like sticking your nose in a slightly burnt strawberry rhubarb pie, according to one imaginative blind taster.

Mouth Instead of continuing with over-the-top jamminess, the wine actually shows some balance in the mouth. There's very light tannin, but a considerable finish.

Design If the Burgundy bottle is Francophile, the wine certainly isn't; it holds no hint of the overt New World character of the wine. Still, it's fun and escapist. If weirdo labels these days are moving in this direction and away from unappetizing animals and irrelevant curse words, then we're all for it.

Dancing Bull Cabernet Sauvignon

$12

Style Heavy New World red
Country California **Vintage tasted** 2006
Grapes Cabernet Sauvignon
Drink with grilled steak, roasted vegetables
Website www.dancingbullwines.com

Unabashedly New World in style, this lush wine is packed with delicious fruit flavors. Thankfully, it doesn't cross the line into being jammy or cloying, and decent acidity and tannins will help it match rather than overwhelm food. We recommend checking out the Dancing Bull website, which is so complex and filled with unexpected features that we felt like we were playing a video game. We can only imagine how cheap this wine would be if the producer didn't have to pay for website development.

Nose Berry aromas dominate, but our blind tasters also found hints of green pepper and a smoky quality.

Mouth Our blind tasters loved the rich black fruit, strong acidity, and mild tannins.

Design It's technically a critter wine, but the rich red background and silhouetted bull won us over. Producers really need to cut down on the red-and-gold motif, though.

Domaine Ste. Michelle Brut

Cuvée • *Two-time Wine Trials selection*

Style Sparkling
Country Washington State **Vintage tasted** Non-Vintage
Grapes Chardonnay, Pinot Noir
Drink with grilled fish, seafood paella
Website www.domainestemichelle.com

This year's winning sparkling wine, Domaine Ste. Michelle has for a second time beat out a host of French Champagnes—including a $150 bottle of Dom Pérignon. Why? Well, it's made in the traditional method of Champagne, and the grapes are from Washington's Columbia Valley, whose climate is similar to that of the Champagne region in France. However, the style is fresher and lighter than Champagne (and drier and better balanced than their own extra dry wine, also recognized in this year's *Wine Trials*). Plus, you're not paying for millions of dollars in PR stunts and glossy magazine ads featuring scantily-clad supermodels.

Nose Fresh aromas of apple, pear, and almond dominate. One taster thought it was a little stinky.

Mouth Like many Champagnes, it's bready and a little spicy, with intense bubbles and impressive balance.

Design The bottle's trying to look expensive, but we know better.

Domaine Ste. Michelle Extra Dry

$12

FINALIST

Style Sparkling
Country Washington State **Vintage tasted** Non-Vintage
Grapes Chardonnay, Pinot Noir
Drink with smoked fish, spicy Thai curries
Website www.domainestemichelle.com

If you're craving sugar in your bubbly, this wine is a great place to start. Confusingly, "extra dry" actually denotes a slightly sweet sparkling wine—if you're looking for something truly dry, try a "brut" wine. That said, this year's extra dry was too sweet for some tasters. Domaine Ste. Michelle is the bubbly arm of the acclaimed Washington State producer Château Ste. Michelle, and their famous attention to value and quality is evident in this delicious offering.

Nose Aromas of straw, yeast, and crisp pear would not be out of place in good French bubbly—but all that sweetness would.

Mouth It's definitely a bit sweet, but the acidity works to keep it in balance—this one is a crowd pleaser.

Design This newly designed look adds a bit of gold gaudiness to an otherwise tasteful bottle. We miss the old version.

Domäne Wachau Grüner Veltliner

Federspiel Terrassen

Style Light Old World white
Country Austria **Vintage tasted** 2007
Grapes Grüner Veltliner
Drink with whole grilled fish, crab claws
Website www.domaene-wachau.at

Located in Austria's beautiful Wachau Valley and overlooking the Danube, Domäne Wachau occupies an enviable piece of land. The wines coming from this producer are wonderful, serving as fitting ambassadors for their as-yet-relatively-unknown region. It's only a matter of time until Grüner Veltliner gets its 15 minutes of fame; wine geeks are already drooling over it.

Nose Punchy, bright, and clean, this wine has interesting aromas of hay and, believe it or not, piña colada. Still, one blind taster said it was lovely and sophisticated.

Mouth A near-effervescence combines with loads of acidity. There's also a strong peach flavor.

Design A very grown-up label for a very grown-up wine coming from a very grown-up producer. The lack of frills is what Grüner Veltliner is all about.

Don Miguel Gascón Malbec

Style Heavy New World red
Country Argentina **Vintage tasted** 2008
Grapes Malbec
Drink with fajitas, beef stew
Website www.gasconwine.com

Imported by the powerhouse E & J Gallo, Gascón manages to produce a distinctive, delicious wine that prompted our blind tasters to write comments like "Savory!" "Wonderful!" and "Delicious!" It even reminded one blind taster of a slightly aged Burgundy—a throwback to the Old World style that once ruled Argentina. In a field of good-value Malbecs, this one stands out for its unique flavors, low price, and earthy, savory allure.

Nose In addition to the usual suspects of fruit, our blind tasters also found aromas of tea leaves, plums, and potpourri.

Mouth Herbal and floral flavors stand out. The notes of cranberry and plum reminded one blind taster of Thanksgiving at home.

Design That central graphic is too ornate for our tastes, but the layout of the label is thoughtful and elegant. All in all, we're inclined to like it.

El Coto de Rioja Crianza
D.O.C.

Style Light Old World red
Country Spain **Vintage tasted** 2005
Grapes Tempranillo
Drink with hearty soups, hard cheeses
Website www.elcoto.com

A relatively young winery (it was founded in the early 1970s), El Coto turns out Riojas that are positively ancient in style. Dusty and leathery, these wines are packed with the sour cherries and barnyard aromas that are part of the classic Rioja profile. We love it, but then, we're suckers for the Old World. If you don't like barnyard—that mulchy, earthy smell typical in Chianti and Rioja—this wine won't be for you.

Nose It's smoky and leathery, with an aroma that reminded one blind taster of oolong tea. That barnyard aroma is unmistakable.

Mouth One blind taster hit it on the head: "sour cherry, earth, acid (in a good way)!"

Design The bottle looks even more ancient than the wine tastes. If the producers would just lose the elk and the crest, it wouldn't be half bad—and besides, no winery founded in 1970 should have a crest in the first place.

El Coto de Rioja Rosado
D.O.C.

 $10

Style Rosé
Country Spain **Vintage tasted** 2008
Grapes Garnacha, Tempranillo
Drink with Manchego cheese, grilled shrimp
Website www.elcoto.com

This fresh, fruity rosé is a nice twist on traditional Spanish Rioja. Made from Garnacha and Tempranillo, the two principal grapes in red Rioja, this wine is tart and refreshing rather than earthy and rich; thankfully, it shares impressive quality and value with its red cousins. It's always fun to see a twist on a classic, but the Rosado's intense acidity and simple fruit flavors are delicious in any case.

Nose Perky citrus blends with berry aromas and a hint of something vegetal. It smells a bit cheap, but then again, it is.

Mouth The intense acidity steals the show here, but our blind tasters picked up green flavors and some banana as well.

Design The label would be better suited to a hunting lodge than a bottle of wine. Still, it's a nice change from the usual critter wine: they at least picked an animal that is majestic rather than adorable.

Erath Pinot Gris

$15

Style Light New World white
Country Oregon **Vintage tasted** 2008
Grapes Pinot Gris
Drink with grilled shrimp, green salad
Website www.erath.com

A New World producer's choice to use the Francophile name for this grape, instead of the increasingly banal Italian name (Pinot Grigio), reflects an ambition to make wines that transcend Pinot Grigio's reputation for pleasant, but very ordinary drinking. Any self-importance on Erath's part is well-earned, as they've managed to produce an interesting, balanced wine at an affordable price.

Nose There's a faint vegetal smell that one taster identified as asparagus, along with plenty of the bright fruit typical in Pinot Gris.

Mouth The flavors are complex and tough to identify, but one blind taster came up with "cactus pads and cat pee." It's steely, too.

Design The slim, tapered bottle and low-key label design are impressive. Interesting fact: the name is an anagram of both "earth" and "heart."

Fairhills Malbec
Fair Trade Certified

Style Heavy New World red
Country Argentina **Vintage tasted** 2007
Grapes Malbec
Drink with pizza, grilled vegetables

This is a Malbec capable of setting a progressive heart aflutter. We're informed that Fairhills benefits more than 1,300 citizens in Argentina, Chile, and South Africa, and that it focuses on "improving the living and social conditions of the producers." As far as we can tell, this wine will single-handedly end world poverty, reverse global warming, and provide healthcare to the Third World. And somehow, the wine itself is still delicious. So go ahead, have a bottle with dinner—do it for the children.

Nose Bright cherry aromas are tempered by a strong herbal note that reminded one taster of Herbal Essences shampoo.

Mouth Berries, herbs, and a bit of olive oil fade into a long finish.

Design Too much going on, with sunbursts, multiple fonts, and wavy colored lines. The tag line "embraced by the wind, kissed by the sea, guided by the stars" sounds like an effective pitch—just not one for wine.

Fat Bastard Chardonnay

Two-time Wine Trials selection

$12

Style Heavy Old World white
Country France **Vintage tasted** 2007
Grapes Chardonnay
Drink with Indian curries, creamy soups
Website www.fatbastardwine.com

In our first edition of *The Wine Trials*, we couldn't understand why a perfectly good French winery would choose to call its wine Fat Bastard. We still can't—but some drinkers seem to love the name, so who are we to judge? The wine itself is excellent, displaying a pleasant thickness, and stuffed with interesting aromas and flavors. If the name bothers you, just wrap the bottle in a brown paper bag. That's what we did.

Nose There's more going on here than in the previous vintage. Bananas, flowers, and tropical fruit all make appearances.

Mouth It delivers on its name: with 13.5% alcohol, this wine feels big and round in the mouth.

Design The hippo—presumably the Fat Bastard himself—perches atop the label. We can't help but find him adorable.

Fetzer Chardonnay
Valley Oaks

Style Heavy New World white
Country California **Vintage tasted** 2008
Grapes Chardonnay
Drink with chicken salad, crab cakes
Website www.fetzer.com

Best of the *Wine Trials* in the heavy white category, Fetzer was a universal hit among our tasters, who were shocked when the brown paper bags came off. The expectation of Fetzer Chard is something big and oaky, but some tasters even thought this might even be Old World. It clearly excited their imaginations as well, reminding them of everything from grapefruit, to citrus, sweet pea blossom to jasmine. Let's hope more California Chardonnays will be made in this style. What a surprise.

Nose It's complex and delightful, with citrus, mineral, and apple aromas.

Mouth There's more fruit here, with mineral and a bit of viscosity. The balance is inspiring.

Design Perhaps the only bad thing about this wine is the bottle—with the ubiquitous vineyard illustration front-and-center on the label, surrounded by predictable flowing script and pale gold trim, the design is painfully ordinary.

Fetzer Gewürztraminer

$9

Valley Oaks

Style Aromatic New World white
Country California **Vintage tasted** 2008
Grapes Gewürztraminer
Drink with Thai green curry, chicken tikka masala
Website www.fetzer.com

Gewürztraminer—it's almost as much fun to say as it is to drink. Aromatic, often sweet, loaded with scents of fruits and flowers and accompanied by a kick of acidity, it's a wine that embodies the spirit of fun. Best of all, it's food-friendly: there's nothing quite like a good Gewürztraminer with Indian or Thai foods.

Nose There's more here than we can possibly identify. Honeysuckle, nectarine, lychee, and honey are just a few of the aromas this wine evokes.

Mouth Several tasters picked up a distinct taste of orange. There's plenty of sugar here, and we might have liked a bit more acidity to complement it.

Design Fetzer labels are just too busy for us. Do they really need a foil stamp over the vineyard? And the pompous script is outdated.

Fetzer Sauvignon Blanc

$9

Valley Oaks

Style Light New World white
Country California **Vintage tasted** 2008
Grapes Sauvignon Blanc
Drink with salad, mild cheeses
Website www.fetzer.com

Many wine drinkers are acidity addicts: there is a rush to a really zingy wine that can't be found anywhere else. This blisteringly acidic wine is just the fix for that kind of junkie. Still, despite a vivacious kick, the wine remains a well-rounded winner. And unlike many of the New Zealand Sauvignon Blancs we tasted, this wine's nose was restrained and mild.

Nose It's frustratingly faint, although there are definitely flowers and grapefruit if you concentrate.

Mouth Besides its mouth-puckering acidity, this wine offers citrus, flowers, and a slightly grassy finish.

Design Once again, a winery puts a picture of a vineyard on the bottle. Is this really necessary? We've never seen a milkshake with a picture of a cow on it.

Finca El Portillo Malbec

Style Heavy New World red
Country Argentina **Vintage tasted** 2008
Grapes Malbec
Drink with steak, mild Indian stews
Website www.bodegasalentein.com

This subtle, expansive wine is a nice contrast with the aggressive, fruity style typical of Argentine Malbecs. That's not to say the wine isn't lush: there's enough red fruit and chocolate to satisfy most drinkers, and it will still pair well with a variety of meat dishes. But it also has distinct character; its unusual, woody flavors delighted our blind tasters and even evoked memories of Christmas.

Nose It's a bit faint, with herbal and pine aromas. Some blind tasters thought of it as green or dewey.

Mouth Classic red fruit and chocolate flavors are complemented by subtle spice and wood. Tannins are definitely there, but they're not overwhelming. The overall effect is understated and expansive—a real treat.

Design The design is as subtle as the wine inside; remove the text and this could be an Abstract Expressionist painting.

Fish Eye Cabernet Sauvignon

Style Heavy New World red
Country California **Vintage tasted** 2006
Grapes Cabernet Sauvignon
Drink with spicy étouffée, chicken tacos
Website www.fisheyewines.com

Fish Eye has its tentacles everywhere, growing as fast as it can, and in all directions—including up: it's the economy-class wine of choice for Continental Airlines (although this particular bottle isn't available on flights—only the Merlot and Chardonnay are). Still, the wines are decent, interesting, and undeniably cheap. Unless you're on an airplane, that is. Better hope you have exact change.

Nose The aromas reminded one blind taster of Cabernet Franc, with intense notes of black pepper, herbs, and berries.

Mouth Aggressive Christmas-like aromas of herbs and potpourri come on pretty strong.

Design The bright colors are fairly garish, and the font goes out of its way to look rustic-hip. It definitely looks cheap. But we'll admit to perking up at the sight of a 187 mL bottle of one of these at 30,000 feet. Or better yet, sneak on a whole 750 in your laptop bag.

Forest Glen Pinot Grigio

California

Style Light New World white
Country California **Vintage tasted** 2008
Grapes Pinot Grigio
Drink with grilled cheese sandwich

This wine reminds us of a decent romantic comedy: it's light, pleasant, and quickly forgotten. It isn't the kind of Pinot Grigio we'll talk about for years to come, but it makes a nice accompaniment for a picnic or an evening in the backyard. That's worth appreciating: we'd go crazy if we always had to watch serious art flicks. There's some sugar in this one, so if you don't like sweet wines, watch out.

Nose Light, aromatic, and fruity. There's something slightly synthetic about it, though, prompting one taster to refer to the aroma as "plastic banana surprise."

Mouth There's apple here, and a refreshing steeliness. Unfortunately, a slightly chemical taste continues to dog the wine.

Design Though we are generally not huge fans of the frolicking animal motif, this bottle's design is elegant and balanced. Except for the awful initial caps.

Francis Ford Coppola Bianco

Style Light New World white
Country California **Vintage tasted** 2008
Grapes Pinot Grigio, Sauvignon Blanc, Chardonnay
Drink with grilled fish, citrus salad
Website www.ffcpresents.com

It may not be a masterpiece on par with *The Godfather*, but this affordable Pinot Grigio blend should still make Francis Ford Coppola proud. More of a summer blockbuster than a serious character study, its flavors of tropical fruit and crisp citrus advertise unpretentious fun. Best of all, you can get a whole bottle for less than the price of a movie ticket. And some free residual sugar to boot.

Nose A distinct aroma of banana dominates, with plenty of lemon underneath. Some tasters found the nose a little weak.

Mouth A round, fat wine, unusually opulent for a Pinot Grigio. But really, what else would you expect from Coppola?

Design The label depicts an old-school movie theater framing a vineyard landscape. Cute, but a bit heavy handed.

Freixenet Cordon Negro Brut

Two-time Wine Trials selection

$9

Style Sparkling
Country Spain **Vintage tasted** Non-Vintage
Grapes Parrellada, Macabeo, Xarel-lo
Drink with smoked salmon, vegetable tempura
Website www.freixenet.com

Freixenet plays off all the sparkling wine stereotypes out there. They would have you believe that only dangerously attractive young people drink it while celebrating a massive bonus or entertaining celebrities at a bottle-service nightclub. And with this wine's yeasty, Champagne-like flavors, it's almost possible to believe the advertising. But don't fear; there's no Freixenet rule against frumpy or non-celebratory drinkers. Which is good, because we enjoy this two-time *Wine Trials* honoree just about anytime.

Nose It has a yeasty aroma that reminded one blind taster of buttered toast, but it's balanced by distinct apple notes.

Mouth There are lemon and apple flavors, along with refreshing acidity and a fresh, clean feeling that made our blind tasters think of wet rocks.

Design The extremely dark Freixenet bottle mysteriously conceals its contents. Some people probably buy it out of mere curiosity.

Freixenet Cordon Negro Extra Dry
Two-time Wine Trials selection

Style Sparkling
Country Spain   **Vintage tasted** Non-Vintage
Grapes Parrellada, Macabeo, Xarel-lo
Drink with hard cheeses, mild curries
Website www.freixenet.com

Know how to pronounce Freixenet? "Fresh-eh-net" (the word is Catalan, as this wine is from Catalunya). This wine may be Spanish, but it could easily be mistaken for a Champagne—its toastiness, earthy aromas, and minerality are distinctly French. It's a brunch wine, and it also works well with slightly spicy foods, as the sweetness creates a nice balance and soothes the mouth.

Nose Rich, toasty aromas blend with intense minerality; the nose suggests a wine much pricier than this one.

Mouth There's sugar here, but it's restrained and not at all cloying. This is an extraordinarily elegant extra dry wine.

Design There's a lot to be said for the black bottle, although it has one major fault: it's tough to see how much wine is left. We suggest just drinking it all.

Fuzelo Vinho Verde

Style Light Old World white
Country Portugal **Vintage tasted** 2008
Grapes Alvarinho, Trajadura
Drink with goat cheese salad, fresh crab

Vinho Verde is all about biting acidity and that slight effervescent prickle, and this wine has plenty of both. High acidity can be an acquired taste, but once you've caught the bug it's like being a roller-coaster fanatic: the bigger the better. Meant for sipping outside on a too-hot summer day, this wine will also fare well with sushi—and its lemon-lime flavors make it a natural fit for a fresh ceviche. The acidity might threaten to strip the enamel off your teeth, but at least you'll have a great time.

Nose Lemon, lime, and flower aromas are unmistakable. Some of our blind tasters also picked up on apple and some Old World minerality.

Mouth The acidity steals the show here, but there are also lemon flavors and even some tropical fruit.

Design It looks like a flower child vomited up this label design. The close-up of the exploding flower looks borderline grotesque, and the shade of green seems sickly.

Gaucho Club Malbec

$10

Style Heavy New World red
Country Argentina **Vintage tasted** 2007
Grapes Malbec
Drink with shepherd's pie, sautéed spinach

"Critter wines" with animals on the label can be found everywhere. But it's not so often that you see the use of human images to sell wine. Gaucho is named after the legendary cowboys who herded livestock in the Southern Cone. It remains to be seen whether gauchos would actually prefer this wine in a blind tasting; underneath the rustic taste, there's a soft, feminine aspect that seems out of keeping with the Gaucho image, but *we're* definitely not complaining.

Nose It has an unusually savory, briny quality that reminded our blind tasters of olives and raisins.

Mouth There's dried red fruit and decent acidity, as well as some soft tannins. It's impressively smooth without being flabby at all.

Design The black-and-white photo of an old Gaucho is a bit kitschy; the entire thing feels a little too exploitative for our taste. And while we like the basic label design, we found the angled text disorienting.

Geyser Peak Cabernet Sauvignon

$15

Style Heavy New World red
Country California **Vintage tasted** 2005
Grapes Cabernet Sauvignon
Drink with lamb kebabs, hard cheeses
Website www.geyserpeakwinery.com

Part of the budget line of the well-respected Geyser Peak Winery (but a splurge by *Wine Trials* standards), this year's winning heavy red wine is a quintessential inexpensive California Cabernet with some tannic backbone to it. Not that there aren't the bold, jammy fruit flavors, too. Still, it's fairly well balanced and feels sleeker in the mouth than you might expect given all the berry aromas. At this price level, managing to balance bold California power with a bit of restraint is an impressive feat.

Nose It's loaded with sweet black fruit that borders on being jammy or even rotten. There's also some spice, which reminded one taster of pumpkin pie.

Mouth It's surprisingly austere given the plush nose, although there's certainly fruit here as well—and age-worthy tannin.

Design Although we like the use of negative space and the restrained fonts, this label manages to seem cheaper than it really is.

Geyser Peak Sauvignon Blanc

$14

Two-time Wine Trials selection

Style Light New World white
Country California **Vintage tasted** 2007
Grapes Sauvignon Blanc
Drink with vegetable tempura, white fish, crab
Website www.geyserpeakwinery.com

Geyser Peak's proclaimed dedication to terroir (see, e.g., their website) is relatively unique at this price point among American producers. It's refreshing to see such a commitment coming from a winery that's churning out hundreds of thousands of cases of wine each year. Perhaps it's all for show, but our blind tasters were still big fans of this bright, summery wine, selecting it this year for the second time. It's ideal for outdoor entertaining or indoor imbibing.

Nose The scents are powerfully aromatic, with orange and the distinct—though not unpleasant—smell of sweat.

Mouth There's a slight prickle on the palate, and an interesting flavor that one blind taster compared to sweet onion.

Design We applaud Geyser Peak's decision to keep it simple and refrain from throwing in a château or curlicue vines. Still, there's something missing here.

Gnarly Head Pinot Grigio

 $11

Style Light New World white
Country California **Vintage tasted** 2008
Grapes Pinot Grigio
Drink with grilled tuna, chicken tacos
Website www.gnarlyhead.com

We get it, Gnarly Head: you're very hip. Though the producers at this young winery have clearly spent far too much time and money trying to brand themselves as cool and relaxed, we have to admit that they make good wines. The makers tend to supercharge all their wines—and while this wine may not be objectively powerful, it's still pretty huge for a Pinot Grigio. Unlike many other Pinot Grigios, which are often accused of being faint and unremarkable, this one bursts with fruit and enough acidity to match it with sushi.

Nose It's full of peaches, bananas, and tropical fruit. It may not be a huge nose, but it's definitely dense.

Mouth Our tasters were impressed by the balanced acidity, hint of salt, and long finish.

Design Points are awarded for gnarlyness: the unusual color scheme, twisting graphic of a grapevine, and bold font mirror the take-no-prisoners approach to wine.

Green Bridge Petite Sirah

$8

Style Heavy New World red
Country California **Vintage tasted** 2007
Grapes Petite Sirah
Drink with juicy steaks, lamb chops

Tannins serve as the backbone of red wines, providing structure, aging potential, roughness, and a slight bitterness to help wines pair with food and keep them from becoming syrupy fruit bombs; they also fade over time and help wines develop as they age. Petite Sirah is famous as an extraordinarily tannic wine, and almost all our tasters made some reference to the heavy tannins in this bottle.

Nose Big floral aromas with a bit of vanilla dominate. One taster described the smell as big and round, another simply as yummy.

Mouth It's an explosion of fruit and tannins—wonderful if you like the style.

Design Well, there's a bridge. The contrast between the hunter green and slate gray is pleasing, and the bold font is reassuring.

Guigal Côtes du Rhône
Two-time Wine Trials selection

$13

FINALIST

Style Heavy Old World red
Country France **Vintage tasted** 2005
Grapes Syrah, Grenache, Mourvèdre
Drink with blue cheese, burgers
Website www.guigal.com

A Guigal wine is generally a safe bet. One of the best-known names in the Côtes du Rhône, Guigal's wines range from the affordable to the astronomical. An attention to quality permeates even the lower price points, resulting in impressive offerings like this two-time *Wine Trials* winner and 2010 finalist for best heavy red. Distinctly Old World, the wine has impressive balance, along with the woody and herbal aromas often present in a good Côtes du Rhône.

Nose The wine is filled with subtle vegetal scents and a hint of pine. It also has some nice floral aromas.

Mouth Our blind tasters found a variety of interesting flavors, including thyme, cedar, and violets. But they mostly agreed it was subtle, balanced, and expressive.

Design The bottle is an amusing mix of old-school French fontage with the new-school desire to evoke a sense of place through nostalgic geographical imagery.

Hahn Estates Cabernet Sauvignon

$14

Central Coast

Style Heavy New World red
Country California **Vintage tasted** 2007
Grapes Cabernet Sauvignon, Merlot
Drink with venison, duck breast
Website www.hahnestates.com

Hahn Estates is a fairly all-encompassing California producer. And they seem to like their fowl—this chicken isn't the only bird they use on their labels. Hahn is the German word for rooster, and as the back label of this wine explains, he is the namesake of the winery, symbolizing their persistence. Pretty big break for a chicken.

Nose A bit of a fruit bomb, this wine has some chemical notes and also some black pepper ones. Ultimately, it smells pretty cheap.

Mouth Interestingly, there are notes of dark chocolate in this full-flavored Cab. The finish is unimpressive, if slightly longer than usual.

Design The lone rooster looks crazed, just like other lone roosters we know. And, really, Estates? Isn't that word a bit pretentious? Then again, this whole label is pretty pretentious.

Hahn Estates Pinot Noir

Monterey

$15

Style Light New World red
Country California **Vintage tasted** 2006
Grapes Pinot Noir
Drink with grilled chicken, baked ham
Website www.hahnestates.com

Pinot Noir grown in California has an entirely different character from that of the same grape in France. Where the French wines are restrained and can seem almost weightless, California Pinots tend to be lush and bursting with red berries. This Monterey Pinot Noir is true to type, with fruit flavors so concentrated and intense that some blind tasters wondered if it was a dessert wine. It might not be subtle, but our blind tasters still thought it was delicious.

Nose There's a cherry aroma that some blind tasters found a bit medicinal. There's also raisin, oak, and, yes, grape juice.

Mouth It's soft, supple, and pleasantly round in the mouth—just what a California Pinot Noir should be.

Design For all its elegance in the bottle, it still manages to exude class on the outside—even with a chicken on the bottle.

Hess Chardonnay
Monterey

Style Heavy New World white
Country California **Vintage tasted** 2007
Grapes Chardonnay
Drink with itself; this wine is clearly meant to stand alone.
Website www.hesscollection.com

When many Americans ask a bartender for a glass of Chardonnay, this is what they're craving. A huge, oaky Chardonnay that tastes like it was slathered in butter, this is exactly the kind of wine that infuriates the ABC (Anything But Chardonnay) crowd. Still, there's a reason this style is so prevalent: its toasty flavors of vanilla, oak, and fruit can really hit the spot.

Nose Oak, oak, and more oak, with butter and toasted corn nuts thrown in for good measure. Underneath the wood, you might find hints of Fuji apple or heather.

Mouth Oak shows up here as well, along with flavors of vanilla and toasted popcorn kernels. A shock of acidity keeps the wine from wandering too far past the line of decency, although several tasters complained that it was a bit thin.

Design The hissing lion, which seems like an unfortunate imitation of a royal crest, ought to be hanging in a British hunting lodge.

House Wine Red

Two-time Wine Trials selection

Style Heavy New World red
Country Washington State **Vintage tasted** 2006
Grapes Cabernet Sauvignon, Merlot, Syrah, Malbec
Drink with pork chops and a fresh field salad
Website www.magnificentwine.com

Were it not for brown bags, we probably never would have tried this wine; a lot of these new trying-too-hard labels tend to suggest sugary plonk. Not here. Even though blind tasters didn't go as gaga for this wine as they did last year, it's still a great bottle. Whereas last year's vintage passed as a dead ringer for a Bordeaux, this year's passes simply as a decent table wine. Not that there's anything wrong with that.

Nose This was blind tasters' least favorite part of the wine. A slightly chemical taste of fertilizer permeated, along with strawberry syrup.

Mouth Things pick up in the mouth, with a complex herbaceousness and decidedly less aggressive flavors.

Design Perhaps it's the Magic-Marker-style aesthetic that's scaring restaurants away from actually pouring this as their house wine. Why must this producer sell itself so short? On the other hand, they know more about wine sales than we do.

Ironstone "Obsession" Symphony $8

Style Sweet New World white
Country California **Vintage tasted** 2007
Grapes Symphony
Drink with lamb vindaloo, Massaman curry
Website www.ironstonevineyards.com

We're not sure this wine inspires obsession, exactly, but it is tasty, and it most certainly does inspire speculation. Our blind tasters were stumped as to what it was—they guessed everything from Gewürztraminer to Orange Muscat. In reality, it's made from the Symphony grape, a cross between Muscat of Alexandria and Grenache Gris. We recommend that you pour a glass and take your own guess.

Nose The aromatic nose, stuffed with striking floral scents, is the definite centerpiece of this wine.

Mouth It's certainly sweet, but decent acidity keeps the richness in check. As one blind taster noted, "it tastes like it smells."

Design It may not be fancy, but the simple color scheme and elegant bottle are pleasing to the eye.

Kaiken Cabernet Sauvignon

$14

Style Heavy New World red
Country Argentina **Vintage tasted** 2007
Grapes Cabernet Sauvignon
Drink with empanadas, awkward social settings
Website www.kaikenwines.com

Kaikenes are wild geese in Patagonia that routine fly back and forth between Argentina and Chile. This winery was begun by a Chilean producer who moved to start a new venture in Argentina, so he named the wine after the geese. Romantic, no?

Nose There are definite overwrought chemical overtones. Underneath them, our blind tasters found the scent of berries. And the color of this wine is very dark—almost black.

Mouth This wine fills the mouth with a puckering quality, owing to the slightly rough tannins. There's also a bit of oak and a slightly sweet, cloying aftertaste. Acidity is a bit too low.

Design The label might be the best thing this wine has going for it— perhaps it can make it taste better. It's very clean and sharp at first glance, but more confusing once you look more closely. The font is nice and looks almost Japanese—this could pass for a sake label.

Kourtaki Mavrodaphne of Patras

Two-time Wine Trials selection

FINALIST

$10

Style Sweet Old World red
Country Greece   **Vintage tasted** Non-Vintage
Grapes Mavrodaphne
Drink with berries, crème brûlée, Raisinets

We imagine this is what sweet wine tasted like a thousand years ago. Rich, raisiny, and rustic, this Greek wine is the kind of thing Odysseus would have had to celebrate his return. Even better, a slight deliberate oxidation means that you can keep the bottle open for a few days and the wine won't change—something you'd have to be crazy to attempt with most non-fortified wines.

Nose It's rich and decadent, with aromas of caramel, raisin, and walnut.

Mouth Our blind tasters loved the silky texture and the flavors of toffee and caramel. The sweetness, alcohol, and oxidation almost trick you into thinking this is a Port wine.

Design It's all cheesy Grecophilia, from the fonts to the gold medallion—can they be serious? At least the balance of white, red, black, and gold is soothing.

La Vieille Ferme Rouge

$8

Côtes du Ventoux AOC • *Two-time selection*

Style Heavy Old World red
Country France **Vintage tasted** 2007
Grapes Grenache, Syrah, Carignan, Cinsault
Drink with onion soup, barbecue chicken
Website www.lavieilleferme.com

This Rhône red certainly does its own thing. While it has plenty of prominent red fruit, there are quirky flavors of blueberries and even cola. There's no mistaking it for an elegant wine, but an abundance of character makes this Old World effort a real treasure. This vintage was a bit less spectacular than the 2006 which appeared in last year's *Wine Trials*, but it's still a great value.

Nose There's red fruit here, and plenty of blueberry. Impressively, two of our blind tasters independently identified the taste of cherry cola.

Mouth It's loaded with vanilla and fruit, although some blind tasters found it slightly cheap or synthetic-tasting.

Design Don't be fooled by the fake French handwriting or the homeliness of the chicken couple flirting on the bottle: the maverick marketing punch of Perrin, the Rhône giant, is behind this big brand.

Lan Rioja Crianza
Two-time Wine Trials selection

Style Light Old World red
Country Spain **Vintage tasted** 2005
Grapes Tempranillo
Drink with something special
Website www.bodegaslan.com

Twelve dollars for this trip to Spain's romantic past? You'd better believe it. Named *Wine Trials* Wine of the Year, this Rioja had our blind tasters fooled into thinking it was one of the tasting's secret ringers. But instead, it turned out to be from Rioja, the kind old uncle of wine regions. It is so exciting to see a wine this earthy, elegant, sophisticated—and resistant to the generic "international" style. In the final tasting, this spectacular bargain bottle easily upset a $78 Pinot Noir by unanimous decision.

Nose There are deep, intriguing aromas of earth, mulch, and sour cherry. Tasters also noticed the scent of tea leaves, a sign that four years of age on the Crianza is starting to yield soft, savory dividends.

Mouth It's a rich mixture of leather, raisin, and herbs. This is the most earthy, evocative wine in the book.

Design Distressed yellow paper creates a nice backdrop for the royal red. It looks dated, but then, so is the region, and we're not complaining.

Le Grand Noir GSM

$10

Cellar Jean d'Albert

Style Heavy Old World red
Country France **Vintage tasted** 2006
Grapes Grenache, Syrah, Mourvèdre
Drink with mushroom risotto, goulash

GSM, short for this classic Southern Rhône blend of Grenache, Syrah, and Mourvèdre, is becoming a popular phrase among wine nerds these days. The blend is gaining traction worldwide, especially in Australia, and it's easy to see why—these three grapes balance each other out nicely. The end product still ends up being quite heavy, though, so don't pair this one with anything particularly delicate.

Nose It's rich, dark, and deep, with notes of sweet spice and clove. One blind taster was bothered by a slightly rubbery smell.

Mouth It comes on a bit strong, but it's balanced by dark chocolate and spice. There's also a mulchy leafiness to it.

Design Seeing "GSM," such a manly sounding blend, written in pink letters makes us giggle, as does the pink foil up top. Shouldn't pink be reserved for rosés? GSM demands a deeper color, like a dark blue.

Le Grand Noir Pinot Noir

Cellar Jean d'Albert

$10

Style Light Old World red
Country France **Vintage tasted** 2008
Grapes Pinot Noir
Drink with bucatini all'amatriciana, fried chicken

Pinot Noir is a famously difficult grape. At its best, in Burgundy and California, it can be transcendent and awe-inspiring. But too often, imperfect weather or poor winemaking creates a wine that is thin and unpleasant. So when we find a serviceable French Pinot for under ten or twelve dollars, we're always excited. No one will call this wine transcendent, but it does a solid job with a difficult grape, and for that we're grateful.

Nose There's stewed fruit and some oak here; the aromas have a distinctly New World feel.

Mouth It's a bit vegetal, but there's dark chocolate and fairly strong tannins as well.

Design The effort's there, but an adorable sheep can't compensate for its ungainly shape and awkward fonts. It makes us think of a Fergus Henderson nose-to-tail restaurant.

Le Grand Noir White

Cellar Jean d'Albert

Style Heavy Old World white
Country France **Vintage tasted** 2007
Grapes Chardonnay, Viognier
Drink with lobster bisque, clam chowder

This French attempt at a critter wine is significantly easier to take than its New World counterparts. Not only did the winemakers provide an adorable sheep on the label, but the wine merges a wonderful nose with refreshing acidity. Which isn't to say it isn't opulent: the extraordinarily aromatic Viognier grape combines with the already powerful Chardonnay to offer enough fruit to satisfy even the most power-hungry drinker.

Nose Given the combination of Viognier and Chardonnay, it's predictably aromatic, with tropical fruit, peaches, pears, and some lime.

Mouth The mouth has a little sweetness to it, but it's cut by great acidity.

Design With the charming sheep and old look, this bottle's almost there but misses on the mixture of fonts and logos. And while the wine's tag line, "being unique," is trite, we're at least grateful it's not spelled "ewe-nique."

Liberty School Cabernet Sauvignon $15

Hope Family Wines • *Two-time Wine Trials selection*

Style Heavy New World red
Country California **Vintage tasted** 2007
Grapes Cabernet Sauvignon
Drink with beef in mushroom sauce, burgers
Website www.libertyschoolwinery.com

Liberty School—for whom this is a repeat appearance in *The Wine Trials*—is a relatively humble California producer whose marketing and PR are refreshingly elementary. You've probably seen these bottles everywhere, but not in that in-your-face, Yellow Tail-ish sort of way. While this year's Cabernet is slightly less sensational than last year's, with less depth on the back end, it remains a solid, balanced wine at a good price.

Nose It has plenty of California fruit, with some cinnamon and cola aromas lurking under the surface.

Mouth Strong tannins balance lush berries—this is a California Cabernet through and through. We are a bit surprised by the shorter than expected finish, though.

Design Simple and relatively understated, it could easily pass for a more expensive bottle—just as it did in a brown bag.

Louis Latour Le Pinot Noir

Two-time Wine Trials selection

Style Light Old World red
Country France **Vintage tasted** 2006
Grapes Pinot Noir
Drink with split pea soup, pork chops
Website www.louislatour.com

If Bordeaux and Napa are the intro courses of wine—relatively easy to understand and indispensable for wine drinkers—then Burgundy is the master class. Its famously confusing appellation system and uneven vintages can baffle even the most devoted student. Thankfully, Louis Latour has provided a cheat-sheet wine for the confused and intimidated: its approachable style (rewarded for the second time in *The Wine Trials*) and easy to-understand labeling should help even the least knowledgeable drinker.

Nose Like many Pinot Noirs, it's heavy on cherries.

Mouth It achieves the blend of lightness and intensity that marks a good Burgundy. There's acid here as well, which should help complement food.

Design We're not huge fans of the script logo, but at least there are no goofy animals or vulgar names here.

Ludovicus DO Terra Alta

Style Heavy Old World red
Country Spain **Vintage tasted** 2008
Grapes Garnacha, Tempranillo, Syrah, Cabernet Sauvignon
Drink with blue cheese hamburger, grilled steak
Website www.vinospinol.com

We're always big believers in the value of Spanish wines. This one comes from a town named Batea, just over the border from the world-class wine region of Priorat. The wine is made from Garnacha, Tempranillo, Syrah, and Cabernet grapes, which gives it full, fruity aromas, a bit of complexity, and tannins big enough to pair with hearty food. We just hope too many drinkers don't catch on to Spain, as we'd miss the unfairly low prices.

Nose It reminded our blind tasters of a Bordeaux blend, with cranberry, cherry, and black pepper aromas. One taster (apparently without malice) even compared it to a Jolly Rancher.

Mouth Currant, coffee, pepper, and spicy flavors mingle with strong tannins that will go well with food.

Design It's simple and businesslike, without any frilly graphics or gimmicks. It looks like a table wine, which it is. And of course, we're fans of the Fearless Critic orange.

Manyana Tempranillo
Cariñena D.O.

$8

Style Light Old World red
Country Spain **Vintage tasted** 2007
Grapes Tempranillo
Drink with lamb-stuffed piquillo peppers, milanesa

Even though Garnacha is the most widely planted grape in Cariñena, a region in the north of Spain, this DO wine is made from the Tempranillo grape. It's a light but lush wine that's easy to drink, and our blind tasters were pleased with the careful balance of fruit and acid. Just don't expect fireworks from this simple bottle.

Nose It's faint, but most noticeable are jammy aromas of plum and cranberry. One blind taster even noticed the smell of bread.

Mouth Nothing spectacular happens here; the light body has dark fruit and decent acidity, but no one was tricked into thinking this bottle was anything but cheap.

Design We can't get on board with this spelling of mañana. This is a wine bottle, not someone's Facebook wall. And the DO label ends up looking tacky, with its oversized advertisement of the wine's Spanish provenance.

Mark West Pinot Noir

California • *Two-time Wine Trials selection*

Style Light New World red
Country California **Vintage tasted** 2007
Grapes Pinot Noir
Drink with roast pork, barbecue chicken
Website www.markwestwines.com

Since their wine last appeared in the first edition of *The Wine Trials*, the revolutionaries at Mark West have continued to fight their Pinot for the People campaign. Their manifesto demands "rich, fruit-inspired, easy-drinking wine." And this lush Pinot is nothing if not easy-drinking. It remains to be seen whether these wines will topple class divisions or foment international uprisings, but we can't wait to see what Mark West's Five-Year Plan has in store.

Nose It's all about the cherry here. Some blind tasters found the nose pleasant and even interesting, while others thought it smelled synthetic.

Mouth Cherry again, which can seem sickly sweet if you're not a fan of jam. The wine showed slightly less earth and balance than last year's edition.

Design This bottle is dangerously bourgeois; the playfulness of the website doesn't translate to the design, which is all business and tasteful maroon.

Marqués de Cáceres White Rioja $10

Two-time Wine Trials selection

Style Light Old World white
Country Spain **Vintage tasted** 2007
Grapes Viura
Drink with risotto, macaroni and cheese
Website www.marquesdecaceres.com

Everybody knows Marqués de Cáceres, either in its white, red, or pink form; it might well be the most widely distributed Spanish brand in the US. (Keep an eye out and you might even find it somewhere as unlikely as a gas station, drugstore, or neighborhood bodega.) This year's effort was a bit less successful than last year's floral, tropical vintage, but it's still a great wine for the price. It's light enough to pair with something as delicate as raw fish, but we recommend drinking it with something more substantial and flavorful.

Nose It's sprightly and vibrant, with lemon-lime aromas and a hint of something vegetal.

Mouth Yep, it's definitely vegetal: one blind taster picked up on the flavor of cabbage.

Design We applaud the screwcap, but this design is getting old. This look definitely works better for red wines. Maybe lay off the gold?

Melini Chianti San Lorenzo

DOCG

Style Light Old World red
Country Italy **Vintage tasted** 2007
Grapes Sangiovese
Drink with spaghetti alla bolognese, game birds

On the whole, our blind tasters had mixed feelings about Chianti. Although many enjoyed the rich flavors and food-friendly acidity, others reacted negatively to a mulchy, almost dirty smell that the wine often gives off. It's that certain scent associated with Chianti; in wine jargon it's described as "barnyard." Some people like it, but those who hate it, *hate* it. While it makes a cameo appearance here, much more obvious are the crowd-pleasing aromas of cherry, spices, and flowers. It's a great choice for barnyard-haters looking for a good pasta wine.

Nose Blind tasters loved the spicy nose packed with red fruit. One taster picked up on the smell of fresh-cut violets.

Mouth The same flavors continue in the mouth, along with a healthy acidity that is just lovely.

Design It's simple and Italian. We're tired of the vineyard-and-crest motif, but at least it's relatively subtle here.

Mezzacorona Chardonnay

$9

Vigneti delle Dolomiti IGT

Style Light Old World white
Country Italy **Vintage tasted** 2008
Grapes Chardonnay
Drink with grilled shellfish, moules frites
Website www.mezzacorona.it

This is the type of wine that makes us loathe even more those over-oaked Chardonnays out there that are redolent of butter, butter, and more butter. A reminder of the great versatility of the grape, Mezzacorona's Northern Italian version is elegant and balanced, combining acid with fruit. See, it can be done! For $9!

Nose Blind tasters picked up on a range of flavors from green apple to oak, citrus to stone fruit. But they all agreed that the aromas were nice and clean.

Mouth Steely and balanced, with substantial acid, this is what a good Old World white should be. And there's a hint of banana to boot.

Design Don't leave this bottle out in the sun. Not only will its contents cook, but you might be blinded if the sun catches the gold the wrong way. The orange is a nice counterbalance, though—better than some of the others in this line.

Mezzacorona Pinot Grigio

Vigneti delle Dolomiti IGT

$10

Style Light Old World white
Country Italy **Vintage tasted** 2008
Grapes Pinot Grigio
Drink with bruschetta, shrimp scampi
Website www.mezzacorona.it

As the largest estate producer of Pinot Grigio in Italy, Mezzacorona isn't exactly a mom-and-pop outfit. They make wine by the book, and you're unlikely to be surprised by anything they have to offer. Still, the book isn't that bad, and you can be confident that their Pinot Grigios will be light, fruity, and undeniably pleasant. Our tasters certainly enjoyed this one: words like clean and toasty kept cropping up, and we all agreed it would make a great apéritif on the porch.

Nose Our tasters enjoyed the balance between the light tropical fruit and citrus on the one hand, and the heavier butter and vanilla aromas on the other.

Mouth It has a toasty feel, with plenty of fruit to match the nose.

Design The makers are trying too hard for class: there's enough gilding on this bottle to cover half of Versailles.

Monte da Cal

$10

Style Heavy Old World red
Country Portugal **Vintage tasted** 2006
Grapes Aragonês, Alfrocheiro, Alicante de Bouschet
Drink with barbecue, Cajun dishes
Website www.daosul.com

Made by Dão Sul, one of the most visible producers in Portugal, this is a wine to sip next to the fireplace. Juicy and chocolatey, with strong tannins to provide balance and a bit of aging potential, it seems much more complex than its price or its origins would suggest. We don't know what this wine will taste like in five years, but with those huge flavors and heavy tannins, it might be worth hiding a few bottles in a closet to find out.

Nose Our tasters picked up on chocolate, raspberry, and a pleasant smokiness.

Mouth The huge tannins, chocolate flavors, and slight spiciness make this wine a keeper. One of our blind tasters even skipped a description and just went with "good!!!!"

Design The hill-shaped label and elegant use of white space make this bottle, like the wine inside, seem much more expensive than it is.

Monte Velho White

$8

Style Light Old World white
Country Portugal **Vintage tasted** 2008
Grapes Roupeiro, Antão Vaz, Perrum
Drink with grilled fish, baked goat cheese
Website www.esporao.com

If you've never heard of Roupeiro, Antão Vaz, or Perrum, you're not alone—these grape varieties are little known in even the most ardent wine geek circles. Indigenous to Alentejo, the Portuguese region where this wine is made, they make bright, aromatic wines with a healthy dose of minerality. Portuguese offerings are often great values, and a complete lack of name recognition has driven down prices even further here—you can grab this refreshing treat for the cost of a couple beers.

Nose It's floral and vibrant, with a distinct smell of orange.

Mouth For a wine with this much aroma, it's bright and fairly light-bodied. There's a nice cut of acidity and a little bit of a prickle as well.

Design We like minimalism, but there's so much negative space that we wondered if the makers had forgotten the rest of the label. Still, it's elegant enough to pass for a $100 bottle.

Montecillo Rioja Crianza

Style Light Old World red
Country Spain **Vintage tasted** 2005
Grapes Tempranillo
Drink with chicken tagine, braised pork
Website www.osborne.es

Like many Old World wine regions, Rioja has exacting legal standards governing winemaking; whether or not a wine qualifies as a Reserva, Gran Reserva, or merely a plain Rioja is dictated by requirements of aging, grape type, and production volume. A Crianza is the second rung up on Rioja's hierarchy, denoting a wine that has been aged for at least two years, with at least one year in oak barrels. This one, from the Osborne empire (whose Solaz we dearly miss), has delicious earthy aromas and the kind of tart acidity that makes it an ideal partner for food.

Nose It's got classic Rioja aromas of sour cherries and earth.

Mouth More cherries and earth, with a burst of acid that went over well with the blind tasters.

Design A red-and-black color scheme, winery crest, flowing script next to block lettering, vineyard illustration, and gold gilding. Clearly, this winery believes we're still in the Spanish Golden Age.

Montes Malbec

Style Heavy New World red
Country Chile **Vintage tasted** 2008
Grapes Malbec
Drink with turkey, short ribs
Website www.monteswines.com

Montes is one of the bigger producers in Chile, and they have multiple lines available on the market. This Malbec is from the Classic Series, which is where most budget wines lurk. The Purple Angel and Montes Cherub lines continue with the celestial theme, but their labels are much edgier than this somewhat staid and simple design. Nonetheless, the juice inside this bottle made our blind tasters happy with its big and bold Malbec flavors.

Nose A strong nose has hints of oak, but loads of bright red fruit, too. The overall effect is pleasing, if aggressive.

Mouth The fruit really shines here, dominating the palate. Decent tannins rein it all in, keeping this wine from becoming the ever-dreaded fruit bomb.

Design The angel is a bit much, but the cursive font for the "classic series" actually does manage to convey class. Imagine that.

Mouton Cadet Bordeaux Rouge

Baron Phillipe de Rothschild • *Two-time selection*

Style Heavy Old World red
Country France **Vintage tasted** 2006
Grapes Cabernet Sauvignon, Cabernet Franc, Merlot
Drink with pork skewers, ham and cheese sandwiches
Website www.bpdr.com

This bottle isn't just ubiquitous in the US; you'll see Mouton Cadet in liquor stores and supermarkets all over the world—even in towns and cities where most wines are virtually impossible to find. As it turns out, this is a good thing for wine-craving travelers. This easy-drinking party wine, appearing for the second time in *The Wine Trials*, is wonderfully light and pleasant.

Nose It's restrained, with red fruit and some green pepper.

Mouth Most of our tasters found it light, almost to a fault; some thought it was a bit thin. Again, red fruit and a vegetal green-pepper flavor dominate.

Design The mutton himself evokes a set of dishware from a home decorating store in middle America. We prefer the 1940s bottles from this historical producer—check them out on the website.

Nathanson Creek Merlot
Two-time Wine Trials selection

Style Light New World red
Country California **Vintage tasted** Non-Vintage
Grapes Merlot
Drink with steak, cheese and crackers

Nathanson Creek is owned by Constellation Wines, the largest wine company in the world. But despite its mass-market origins, this Merlot is interesting and thoroughly enjoyable; our blind tasters raved about it both this year and the last. It's a good entry-level wine for the new drinker, and it will go well with everything from chicken dishes to steak.

Nose Our blind tasters identified green vegetal aromas, as well as something distinctly meaty that one taster called sultry.

Mouth The vegetal flavors and berries continue. The impressively firm tannins would go wonderfully with a steak.

Design We love the unique shape: it's stylish, and there's more weight in the bottle than you usually get for this price.

Nobilo Sauvignon Blanc

$14

Two-time Wine Trials selection

Style Light New World white
Country New Zealand **Vintage tasted** 2008
Grapes Sauvignon Blanc
Drink with grilled duck breast, baked ham
Website www.nobilo.co.nz

Appearing for the second time in *The Wine Trials*, Nobilo was founded in the 1940s by a Croatian immigrant whose family had been making wine in Europe for hundreds of years. According to the story, he moved to New Zealand in hopes of continuing to make wines in the Old World style—the likes of which were nowhere to be found in Kiwi country. The only problem is that the flavors in this wine have almost nothing to do with that story. In fact, many of our blind tasters recognized it as a New Zealand Sauv Blanc from a mile away. The only European thing about this wine is its high acidity; otherwise, the Nobilo's tropical, heavy-handed flavors are very New World. Still, it's tart and refreshing, like it should be.

Nose It's less harsh and vegetal than some Sauvignon Blancs, but there's still a hint of what one taster identified as cabbage. And of course, there's grapefruit—lots and lots of it.

Mouth The acidity comes on strong, in a good way. There's a slight prickle as well, and a pleasantly long finish.

Design It's simple and unusually refined for the New World, with a pleasing color combination and regal fonts.

Norton Cabernet Sauvignon

$11

Bodegas Norton

Style Heavy New World red
Country Argentina **Vintage tasted** 2008
Grapes Cabernet Sauvignon
Drink with beef stew, pumpkin pie
Website www.norton.com.ar

Congratulations, Norton! With four wines in this year's edition of *The Wine Trials*, Bodegas Norton has received our Winery of the Year Award. Located in Luján de Cuyo in Mendoza, this British-Swiss-run winery is producing some of the most widely available Argentine wines in the US market. Combine that with their booming enotourism business, and you can't question their winemaking skills—or their marketing savvy.

Nose There are the requisite vegetal aromas associated with Cabernet Sauvignon, along with some deep, dark fruit aromas.

Mouth Expansive. This wine explodes on the palate with juicy fruit and lovely herbal notes.

Design Simple as can be. The design is elegant and understated. Bodegas Norton doesn't need an army of animals to catch consumers' eyes from the shelves.

Norton Malbec

Bodegas Norton

Style Heavy New World red
Country Argentina **Vintage tasted** 2008
Grapes Malbec
Drink with steak au poivre, meatloaf
Website www.norton.com.ar

These days, the connection in many consumers' minds between Argentina and Malbec is indelible. Known as the quality grape from a bargain region, Malbec has made a New World name for itself. Its origins are actually in France, in the Cahors region, where inky black wines are made primarily from Malbec. Its Argentine incarnations are usually big, tannic, and they practically call out to be eaten with a big juicy steak.

Nose The nose has lots of dark fruit, and you might get a whiff of alcohol. (But at 13.5%, it's still considerably weaker than some of the big reds coming out of California.)

Mouth Tannic and rich, with a decently long finish.

Design It's boring, but in a good way. There's nothing for us to pick on, and we most certainly don't mind being nice.

Norton Merlot

Bodegas Norton

$11

Style Heavy New World red
Country Argentina **Vintage tasted** 2008
Grapes Merlot
Drink with Ethiopian food, molten lava cake
Website www.norton.com.ar

The red wines of Bodegas Norton absolutely shone this year, with three wines among the top scorers. This Merlot is the more understated of Norton's single-varietal line, with softer, more supple, less aggressive flavors than the Malbec and Cabernet Sauvignon. It's an easy-to-drink New World red, and it's not too often that you see that, especially at this price point.

Nose Delicate aromas of muddled black fruits were noticed by our blind tasters.

Mouth This Merlot has a softer body than the other Nortons. The tannins were less harsh, which really pleased some blind tasters.

Design This bottle speaks softly and carries a big stick. Practically indistinguishable from Norton's other "Young Varietal" bottles, it exudes the same simplicity (indifference, even?) and elegance. No circus animals here.

Norton Torrontés

$11

Bodegas Norton

Style Aromatic New World white
Country Argentina **Vintage tasted** 2008
Grapes Torrontés
Drink with dessert, vanilla custard
Website www.norton.com.ar

We're more than happy to include this Torrontés, as we find the grape to be an interesting one that deserves more attention that the paltry amount it currently gets. Wines made from Torrontés grapes tend to be on the aromatic side of things, but they're rarely big and flabby in the off-putting way that sweet wines can be. This one weighs in at 13% alcohol— a bit high, but by no means brushing against the ceiling.

Nose Very aromatic, with hints of orange blossom. Multiple blind tasters smelled peach.

Mouth The wine's thick, unctuous body led a couple of blind tasters to incorrectly identify this as a Gewürztraminer. Decent acidity does a good job binding it together.

Design This is the most zippy of Norton's very restrained bottles. The green color of the glass adds some spunk without taking away any of the sophistication these wines are known for.

ÖKO Red

 $10

Style Heavy Old World red
Country France **Vintage tasted** 2006
Grapes Cabernet Sauvignon, Merlot
Drink with beef tenderloin, roast duck

Even in the hippie-filled world of winemaking, this French "eco-wine" from the Languedoc region stands out for its ostentatious granola attitude. The producer's website informs us that ÖKO comes from the phonetic spelling of "ecology," which they take time to define for those of us who missed fourth grade as "the interrelationship of organisms in the environment." Thankfully, the producers didn't neglect quality in their pursuit of ECOCERT organic ratings: the wine is juicy and floral, without the dip in quality that sometimes accompanies budget organic wines.

Nose There's so much red fruit here that one blind taster compared it to a Jolly Rancher.

Mouth It follows through with more cranberry and cherry, although there's enough acidity and tannin to mark it as an Old World wine.

Design It certainly doesn't look French; the massive metallic tree and curving leaves on the bottle neck have a New World enthusiasm and lack of restraint.

ÖKO White

$10

Style Light Old World white
Country Italy **Vintage tasted** 2008
Grapes Pinot Grigio
Drink with seafood, light pastas

Some winemakers claim that organic growing methods make for a subtler wine, and they may be right. Something has to explain the impressive balance and complexity of this Pinot Grigio. This wine won't bowl you over with fruit and body; instead, it introduces itself politely and rewards attention. And as one of the lightest Pinot Grigios on our list (it clocks in at only 12% alcohol), it's a perfect wine to sip all afternoon.

Nose It's gentle, with floral aromas and a bit of citrus.

Mouth The balance is impressive, and the acidity is lively and refreshing. The flavor could last a bit longer, though.

Design Although we like the vague hippieness, the twisting tree and leaf motif is too busy, but at least it looks nice against the pale yellow wine.

Oyster Bay Sauvignon Blanc

$13

Two-time Wine Trials selection

Style Light New World white
Country New Zealand **Vintage tasted** 2008
Grapes Sauvignon Blanc
Drink with fish and chips, grilled shrimp
Website www.oysterbaywines.com

One of the best-known and most popular Kiwi wines, Oyster Bay is like a caricature of New Zealand Sauvignon Blanc, with those flavors often described in the jargon as "gooseberry and elderflower." We'll refrain from using those words, as we know few people who have actually smelled either of the above. Instead, our tasters described it as punchy, vegetal, and clean. It's the essence of the New Zealand style, so if you like Kiwi Sauv Blancs, this wine is for you.

Nose There's plenty of grapefruit here, and a strong vegetal note that reminded our blind tasters of cabbage or Brussels sprouts.

Mouth More vegetal flavors accompany the crisp, tart acidity that screams New Zealand.

Design The label seems to be influenced by Hallmark sympathy cards. A black-and-white bay—more of a cove, really—sits quietly behind tacky calligraphy. The only thing missing is Für Elise.

Parallèle 45 Rosé
Paul Jaboulet Aîné • *Two-time selection*

$13 WINNER

Style Rosé
Country France **Vintage tasted** 2008
Grapes Grenache, Cinsault, Syrah
Drink with summer salads, ceviche
Website www.jaboulet.com

A powerhouse in France producing wines in most of the Rhône Valley appellations, Paul Jaboulet Aîné has ventured into the lower-priced everyday market with their Parallèle 45 line. They seem to have struck a chord with US consumers looking for cheap French wines. Our blind tasters, who previously selected Jaboulet's Côtes du Rhône Blanc and this year also enjoyed the Rouge. This proper summer Southern-France-style rosé was fruity and refreshing enough to win it a Best of *Wine Trials* award.

Nose Bright fruit aromas of banana and strawberry dominate.

Mouth There's citrus, and floral flavors lacking in many rosés. Above all, it's light and refreshing.

Design Jaboulet has replaced the classic French label with a well-conceived version that fuses the new with the old. The bottle deftly avoids busy graphics and stays elegant.

Parallèle 45 Rouge

Paul Jaboulet Aîné

$13

Style Heavy Old World red
Country France **Vintage tasted** 2007
Grapes Grenache, Syrah
Drink with roast chicken, cheese plate
Website www.jaboulet.com

In the last two editions of *The Wine Trials*, Parallèle 45 has appeared in its rouge, blanc, and rosé incarnations—and given that those are the only three wines in the line, that's fairly impressive. As one might expect from the budget wine of a respected producer, this Côtes du Rhône red is simple but well balanced. It has that Old World acidity which seems to deter many new wine drinkers but is perfect for adding structure and helping the wine stand up to food.

Nose The wine's berry-and-barnyard aroma could easily be mistaken for a Burgundy.

Mouth It's impressively balanced, with strong tannins, sharp acidity, and lush flavors.

Design We're more impressed each time we look at this bottle. With its well-conceived fonts and simple design, this is a bottle you can proudly pour at your next dinner party. Anyone remember those ugly old Parallèle bottles from a few years back?

Parducci Sustainable Red

$10

Two-time Wine Trials selection

Style Heavy New World red
Country California **Vintage tasted** 2005
Grapes Merlot, Cabernet Sauvignon, Syrah, Zinfandel
Drink with brownies, pecan pie, chocolate-covered peanuts
Website www.mendocinowinecompany.com

As the name implies, these people are committed to sustainable winemaking—perhaps at the cost of consistency. Whereas last year our blind tasters loved the wine's vegetal aromas, it seems that this year Syrah and Zinfandel took the driver's seat, making the wine fruity and syrupy. We definitely prefer the previous vintage, but this one is still a safe bet. And it's nice to know that you're doing your part to promote sustainable practices.

Nose Very jammy, it smells a bit cheap, and it's slightly cloying. Tasters even noticed a cherry cola-like quality.

Mouth Oddly, the fruit doesn't carry over, and there isn't much on the mouth—just a bit of herbaceousness. The finish is weak and slightly bitter, but the wine shows decent balance.

Design The tree-like vine is lovingly rendered—the idea, of course, is to imagine that it's from one of the family-owned farms where the Sustainable Red's grapes are grown.

Pascual Toso Chardonnay

$13

Style Heavy New World white
Country Argentina **Vintage tasted** 2009
Grapes Chardonnay
Drink with fried fish, Indian curries
Website www.bodegastoso.com.ar

Argentina was one of the stars of this year's *Wine Trials*. With 21 wines among the top 150, it is one of the best represented regions in the book. Pascual Toso, located in Argentina's darling Mendoza region, is a producer whose wines are representative of the style of the region, and this Chardonnay carefully toes the line between unbridled New World enthusiasm and Old World restraint—much like the country of Argentina itself.

Nose The nose is oaky, but still sprightly and limey enough. One blind taster got a whiff of something chemical.

Mouth There's more oak here, but not too much, and it's tempered by a healthy dose of acid. There's even a slight prickle.

Design Bright and sunny, with glistening touches of silver, this wine is very pleasing to the eye. The use of sharp angles makes the whole operation look clean and uncluttered.

Pascual Toso Malbec

Style Heavy New World red
Country Argentina **Vintage tasted** 2008
Grapes Malbec
Drink with red-sauce pastas, lamb sausage
Website www.bodegastoso.com.ar

Aside from this line of single-varietal wines, Pascual Toso produces some sparkling wines and a high-end line, Magdalena Toso, whose bottles are priced well above the cut-off for this guide. There's also a Malbec rosé, whose color is a radioactive hot pink, not the pale salmon color one looks for in a rosé. We'll stick with this Malbec—it's not the most special bottle out there, but it comes into its own with some grilled meat.

Nose Its straightforward fruit aromas smell a bit cheap, and one blind taster identified a bothersome synthetic smell.

Mouth It's inoffensive, with some throwaway fruit aromas and a tiny hint of tannin that fades away to a short finish.

Design An elegant bottle, it looks like it's concealing some important contents. The smart design is something you would expect of a more expensive wine, but we all know that money doesn't buy class.

Pascual Toso Sauvignon Blanc

Style Light New World white
Country Argentina **Vintage tasted** 2009
Grapes Sauvignon Blanc
Drink with gnocchi with cream sauce, fried oysters
Website www.bodegastoso.com.ar

The classic New Zealand Sauvignon Blanc flavor profile is an aggressive one, marked by easily recognized sharp aromas that bowl you over and come accompanied by searing acidity. It's an enjoyable style, but not one that has all that much variability. That's why we're excited by this Argentine Sauvignon Blanc, whose complex flavors of stinky cheese are a definite departure from the norm. The acidity is still there, but it's not so sharp.

Nose Blind tasters were amused by this wine's interesting array of aromas. Among those mentioned were stinky cheese, moss, dust, cabbage, and peach.

Mouth There's a surprising softness given the acidity here, and a taste of cheese rind.

Design The carefully selected colors go nicely together, and even complement well the hue of the wine itself. This color scheme definitely looks better with Pascual Toso's whites than with its reds.

Paul Valmer Merlot

Style Light Old World red
Country France **Vintage tasted** 2007
Grapes Merlot
Drink with pot roast, creamy pastas

$5

BARGAIN

Merlot has had a bad reputation ever since the release of the film *Sideways*. It's partly deserved: the glut of mediocre, fruit-forward, structureless Merlots can sometimes be overwhelming. We can certainly understand why someone might be inclined to write off the whole grape. But that would be a mistake, since good Merlot can be distinctive, interesting, and thoroughly enjoyable to drink. This French entry is definitely on the better end of the spectrum (especially for a budget wine); our blind tasters loved its herbal aromas, rich berries, and strong tannins. So if you've sworn off Merlot, come back and give it a second chance.

Nose It's full of coffee, herbs, and soft berries—fairly complex for a budget Merlot.

Mouth It's huge for this type of wine, with tannins powerful enough to stand up to a juicy steak.

Design This bottle isn't the belle of the ball, but it's $5. 'Nuff said.

Pirovano Barbera
Oltrepò Pavese DOC

Style Light Old World red
Country Italy **Vintage tasted** Non-Vintage
Grapes Barbera
Drink with artichoke pizza, penne all'arrabbiata
Website www.vinicantinepirovano.com

Barbera is just beginning to receive the popularity it deserves. It's a lightish, fruity grape, usually found in Piedmont but often overshadowed by the region's more prestigious Barolo and Barbaresco wines. This wine isn't Piedmontese, though—it's actually from Lombardy, near Pavia, between Milan and Genoa, where plays its own pleasant tune, freed from the shackles of Piedmontese prestige.

Nose There's sour cherry, earthy aromas typical of Italian wine, and some young, fresh vegetality.

Mouth More fruit, along with cocoa and vivacious acidity that will help it pair with tomato-based sauces.

Design The label looks like the cover of a music album; those men are either going to grow grapes or break into three-part harmony—it's hard to tell which. To make room for their portraits, the name of the winery and other vital information are squeezed into the corner—very strange. But admirably modern.

Pirovano Prosecco

$15

Style Sparkling
Country Italy **Vintage tasted** Non-Vintage
Grapes Prosecco
Drink with light cheese and crackers, by itself
Website www.vinicantinepirovano.com

This sparkling wine is crisp and unabashedly fun. Prosecco has acquired a reputation as the poor man's Champagne, but at their best these wines offer a simpler, more appley alternative to their French counterparts—perfect for picnics, evenings on the porch, or simple meals when the depth of a Champagne would be overkill. This bottle is sure to put a smile on your face and make you long for an afternoon in the summer Italian sun.

Nose It's simple and pleasant, with plenty of green apple and a bit of citrus.

Mouth Most blind tasters found this wine wonderfully crisp. A few hair-splitters found the bubbles coarse and inelegant, but the refreshing acidity fixed all faults.

Design That blue print background can induce migraines—maybe if you look at it cross-eyed, a *Magic Eye* image will pop out? Add in a garish crest, a busy border, and strangely spaced text, and this label turns impressively bad.

Pirovano Sangiovese di Romagna
DOC

$9

Style Light Old World red
Country Italy **Vintage tasted** Non-Vintage
Grapes Sangiovese
Drink with pizza, lasagne alla bolognese
Website www.vinicantinepirovano.com

Sangiovese is the grape responsible for many of Italy's greatest wines: it plays a starring role in Chianti, in the controversial Brunello di Montalcino, and in a lot of extremely expensive Super-Tuscans. But the region of Romagna, toward the eastern coast of north-central Italy, is one of the unsung heroes of Sangiovese. It flourishes in the hilly, foggy farmland, generating wines of great balance and depth—if not a lot of power. For us, the acidic, earthy wines this grape produces are the essence of the Italian style.

Nose Our blind tasters loved the soft red fruit aromas and rich scent of earth, along with some classic Italian mulch.

Mouth It's distinctly Old World in style, with cherries, earth, good acidity, and a slight herbal flavor. No big tannins here—this is a wine for drinking immediately.

Design Not exactly the fashionable Italians' best work. What's with the oddly shaped crescent?

Pisato Montepulciano d'Abruzzo

Style Light Old World red
Country Italy **Vintage tasted** 2007
Grapes Montepulciano
Drink with smoky cheeses, chili

This wine is refreshingly modern, in that it isn't affected by the funky aromas that plague some Italian wines. It presumably has something to do with the facility in which the wine is vinified, but we'd like to think the organically grown grapes play a part, too.

Nose A bit faint. It takes a long time to open up, so uncork it a few hours before you plan to drink the wine; don't buy into the myth that only expensive wine needs time to breathe. After a couple of hours, red berry aromas will start to come out.

Mouth It's light bodied with good acidity and not as much of the barnyard aromas that you might expect from this region. The wine is made in a clean manner, but it's on the metallic, slightly chemical side for an Italian red.

Design It's hard not to laugh at a bottle that features an image of the leaning tower of Pisa (which, by the way, has nothing to do with the lovely, humble, rural region of Abruzzo). At least we're spared the classic tourist pose: someone standing as if they're single-handedly holding the building up.

Presto Prosecco
Two-time Wine Trials selection

$10

Style Sparkling
Country Italy **Vintage tasted** Non-Vintage
Grapes Prosecco
Drink with green salads, simple seafood pastas

Flowery, crispy, and festive, this Italian sparkler wowed our blind tasters for the second time in a row. Fruity and refreshing, it prompted one taster to call it mouthwatering and well-balanced; it's everything an inexpensive Prosecco should be. And with its remarkably low alcohol level, it's ideal as an apéritif.

Nose It has distinct floral aromas and plenty of citrus—our blind tasters loved it.

Mouth The impressive balance between lush apricot flavors and tart acidity makes for a refreshing bubbly.

Design What a pretty bottle. We love its voluptuous shape, sparse verbiage, and restrained look—no starbursts or coats-of-arms here. Plus, it's hard for us not to like the color of the label: Fearless Critic orange.

Quinta do Encontro

Style Heavy Old World red
Country Portugal **Vintage tasted** 2004
Grapes Baga, Merlot
Drink with strong cheese, stewed beef
Website www.daosul.com

We're always on the lookout for interesting wines from lesser-known regions, so when we pulled the brown bag off this bottle we were thrilled to see both the price and the origin of this delicious wine. Like the Monte da Cal, this winery is owned by the Portuguese company Dão Sul—clearly a producer to keep an eye on. Big and funky on the nose and luscious on the mouth, this wine has more than enough going on to keep us coming back for more.

Nose This wine is definitely old world; it's funky and even stinky. One blind taster thought it tasted like, um, well, manure. But not in a bad way.

Mouth Dark berries, a rich mouth feel, and coffee flavors pleased our tasters.

Design It's fun, quirky, and unpretentious—just like the wine inside.

Red Truck Petite Sirah

Two-time Wine Trials selection

Style Heavy New World red
Country California **Vintage tasted** 2007
Grapes Petite Sirah
Drink with duck breast, mushroom soup
Website www.redtruckwine.com

This wine's marketing pitch has a lot of Americana to it—which is why we were amused to learn that the winemaker is of Greek-Italian descent. Maybe that explains his pleasantly restrained winemaking style. While last year's vintage was earthy, with hints of sweet spice, this year's version has much more fruit. There is still a heavy dose of tannin, just as there was last year.

Nose The citrus-like aromas reminded one blind taster of a white wine.

Mouth Many found it to be too tannic, while another blind taster guessed it was a Napa Cab.

Design It looks like *The Grapes of Wrath* has gone glamorous. No crop-ruining dust storms here—just sunny California days and concentrated Petite Sirah.

René Barbier Mediterranean White

$6

Style Light Old World white
Country Spain **Vintage tasted** Non-Vintage
Grapes Xarel-lo, Macabeo, Parrellada
Drink with tapas, fish in cream sauce
Website www.renebarbier.com

Despite being Spanish and still, this wine has many of the classic characteristics of a good Champagne: it struck our tasters as doughy and yeasty, and it has a wonderfully acidic bite. It may not be a true substitute for a good glass of bubbly, but it will still make a delicious brunch wine or an accompaniment to tapas. And while you won't impress anyone as a big spender (it's one of the least expensive wines on our list), you can win points by rattling off the three grapes in this Catalan wine—Xarel-lo, Macabeo, and Parrellada.

Nose Honey and a bready, doughy scent are consistent themes in our blind tasting notes.

Mouth Round flavors of honey end in a bright burst of acidity that leaves you ready for another bite of food.

Design The lone seaside chair and sunset have nostalgic meaning to Robin: this was the wine with which his high school friend Meg taught him to drink—and to live well.

Robert Mondavi Pinot Noir
Two-time Wine Trials selection

$11

Style Light New World red
Country California **Vintage tasted** 2007
Grapes Pinot Noir
Drink with grilled chicken, simple ham dishes
Website www.rmprivateselection.com

To some, Robert Mondavi was a viticultural hero who demonstrated California's potential and ushered in a bold new era of powerful, exciting wines; to others, he was a soulless businessman who helped erase stylistic idiosyncrasies in the wine world and create a single homogenous style. Regardless, this Pinot Noir is stuffed with the kind of rich flavors that made Mondavi's reputation. It's a wonderful example of an inexpensive wine in the "international" style.

Nose The aromas include plenty of black fruit and berries, vanilla, and toasty aromas. There's even a quality that one blind taster compared to the smell of roasting pig fat.

Mouth It has an extremely round texture that could easily be mistaken for a Super-Tuscan or a Bordeaux blend. The finish lingers pleasantly.

Design Don't cheapen good wine with bad labels. Do away with the Italianate Mondavi villa shrouded in clouds and silly-looking calligraphy.

Rock Rabbit Sauvignon Blanc

($10)

Central Coast

Style Light New World white
Country California **Vintage tasted** 2008
Grapes Sauvignon Blanc
Drink with light sandwiches, simple green salads
Website www.rockrabbitwinery.com

Rock Rabbit wants so desperately to be a Southern Hemisphere wine. They aim to emulate a New Zealand Sauvignon Blanc with this bottle, and an Australian Shiraz with their Syrah (yes, apparently some producers really do aspire to create wines the likes of Aussie Shiraz). This one has the pickled aromas and tart flavors of a Sauv Blanc from down under, but there is also an interesting spiciness here. So it's a win-win situation; they achieved their goal, and we get a little something extra, too.

Nose Briny aromas of pickle juice mingle with cardamom and exotic spice.

Mouth The briny flavors continue, along with some citrus, some tartness, and medium acidity—but it's nothing like New Zealand acidity. The wine is fruity, but interesting and surprisingly round.

Design The asymmetry of the label is pleasing, even if the sickly green color is not. And the bouncy rabbit's energy seems contagious.

Rodney Strong Sauvignon Blanc

$15

Charlotte's Home

Style Light New World white
Country California **Vintage tasted** 2008
Grapes Sauvignon Blanc
Drink with raw oysters, salade Niçoise
Website www.rodneystrong.com

One of the largest Sonoma County producers, Rodney Strong consistently puts out solid, pleasant wines for a good value. Drinking this Sauvignon Blanc is a bit like having apple juice—but tart, refreshing, aromatic, and alcoholic apple juice. All of which sounds pretty good to us.

Nose Intense apple smells dominate. One perceptive blind taster caught a whiff of oak: while oak is not normally used for Sauvignon Blancs, a small percentage of these grapes were fermented in oak barrels.

Mouth It's less over the top than many New World Sauvignon Blancs, but there are still plenty of flavors of spice and vanilla. The acid is tart and refreshing, but like the rest of the wine, it doesn't go too far.

Design With its beige color scheme and picture of rolling vineyard land, the design is typical California. We like the framing effect for the central graphic, though.

Rosemount Shiraz

Diamond Label • *Two-time Wine Trials selection*

Style Heavy New World red
Country Australia **Vintage tasted** 2006
Grapes Shiraz
Drink with meatloaf, short ribs
Website www.rosemountestate.com.au

Ever seen the Rosemount TV commercials? Borrowing heavily from luxury car ads, they feature sleek, sexy wine bottles from all angles. Yum. Making it into the pages of *The Wine Trials* for the second time in a row, Rosemount is a classic Australian Shiraz: cooked flavors, jammy fruit, and dark chocolate dominate. Still, it's fairly well balanced and lacks the abominable sweetness of most of its kin. If you insist on going for a cheap Aussie Shiraz, we recommend this one.

Nose It's definitely jammy, with sour cherry aromas at the forefront.

Mouth There's plenty of the dark chocolate and intense fruit typical in an Aussie Shiraz. But as one blind taster said, it's surprisingly balanced for a fruit bomb.

Design Rosemount's signature square-bottomed bottle shape ensures that it won't go unnoticed on the shelves. Sexy or not, there's something sinister and threatening about all that black.

Round Hill Cabernet Sauvignon

$8

Rutherford Wine Company

Style Heavy New World red
Country California **Vintage tasted** 2008
Grapes Cabernet Sauvignon, Merlot, Zinfandel, Syrah
Drink with smothered chicken, pepperoni pizza
Website www.rutherfordwine.com

This is a first for the Rutherford Wine Company. Last year we blind tasted a few of their wines, but none of them scored high enough for inclusion in our guide, mainly because our tasters found many to be too sweet. But it looks like they've reined in that style this year, and for that we're happy. In fact, many US producers' wines seemed a bit more in check this year. Let's hope the trend continues—we certainly didn't want it to keep on the way it was going.

Nose It smells cheap and grapey, with some vanilla and what one blind taster described as blackberry crumble.

Mouth A little bit green, a little bit sweet. There's also some nice big blackberry. The finish leaves a lot to be desired.

Design The orange label provides a friendly contrast to the über-dark bottle, and the big round font is still approachable. Like the wine.

Ruffino Aziano Chianti Classico

DOCG

Style Light Old World red
Country Italy **Vintage tasted** 2007
Grapes Sangiovese, Cabernet Sauvignon, Merlot, Canaiolo
Drink with truffle fries, roast chicken
Website www.ruffino.it

Ruffino is the powerhouse of Italian Chianti. This year we blind tasted quite a few of their wines, and this one emerged as the clear favorite. Tasters loved its rustic simplicity; many remarked that they would be happy to have it at their dinner table. We would, too.

Nose The aromas are faint, but our blind tasters picked up on clove and sweet spice.

Mouth This is a very simple but decent wine with sufficient tannins and flavors of wood and berries.

Design It's Italian all the way, from the light pink background to the stone farmhouse. And the use of negative space is nice, too, creating perspective.

Saint Clair Sauvignon Blanc

$15

Vicar's Choice

Style Light New World white
Country New Zealand **Vintage tasted** 2008
Grapes Sauvignon Blanc
Drink with shrimp, scallops, sea bass
Website www.saintclair.co.nz

We were a bit turned off by a website that described the wine in corporate-ese, calling it "a lifestyle range with a light-hearted brand personality." Still, the wine itself is easy to like. Even by the standards of the other New Zealand Sauv Blancs in our tasting, this wine is bold and tropical—a style which is one of our guilty pleasures. We're always happy to have a glass of this—after the first fresh sip, we'll humor the producer's bit about "promoting synergies."

Nose A classic nose of grass, grapefruit, and lemon. One blind taster found it a bit synthetic.

Mouth Vibrantly acidic and well balanced, this wine tastes like it smells.

Design We weren't sure what they were going for here—rings of Saturn? '80s nightclub? '70s roller rink? Whatever the intention, there's way too much going on.

Santa Cristina

Antinori, Toscana IGT • *Two-time selection*

Style Light Old World red
Country Italy **Vintage tasted** 2007
Grapes Sangiovese, Merlot
Drink with red-sauce pasta, Wiener schnitzel
Website www.antinori.it

Antinori was an early popularizer of Super-Tuscans—pricey blends of traditional Tuscan Sangiovese with easy-drinking international grapes intended to make highly concentrated, distinctly un-Italian wines. For the second edition in a row, the Antinori winemakers have proved it possible to create an inexpensive Super-Tuscan that doesn't fall victim to over-fruitiness; this wine marries Sangiovese earthiness and acidity with the approachability of French varietals. Some of the flavors and aromas are frankly a little weird, but we'd rather have than over-extraction.

Nose One blind taster identified the chocolate and cherry aromas as like cherry cordial. Meanwhile, there's a swampy, mossy note underneath.

Mouth Our tasters were intrigued by the liveliness of the mouth.

Design Everything's pretty straightforward and restrained on this bottle. At least they avoided anything obviously ugly.

Santa Ema Chardonnay

Selected Terroir

Style Heavy New World white
Country Chile **Vintage tasted** 2008
Grapes Chardonnay
Drink with fried catfish, insalata Caprese
Website www.santaema.cl

Chile, like Argentina, is thought of by many bargain-conscious consumers as an "it" region. It makes sense that wines coming from South America would be cheaper than their counterparts in California; land costs less, as does labor, among other things. And as far as Chardonnay goes, the Casablanca Valley is a cool climate, ensuring that the wines aren't big, knock-you-over-the-head specimens. See—the stars have aligned to produce cheap Chards like this one.

Nose Most blind tasters report that grape and peach dominate, but one taster smelled beeswax.

Mouth A healthy dose of acid counterbalances the inherent sweetness.

Design The golden-wine-against-red-label color scheme works, but there's a bit too much gilded edge going on around the nameplate. Still, it's reasonably elegant and certainly inoffensive, looking neither cheap nor expensive.

Santa Ema Sauvignon Blanc

$10

Selected Terroir

Style Light New World white
Country Chile **Vintage tasted** 2008
Grapes Sauvignon Blanc
Drink with grilled cheese sandwich, sautéed rapini
Website www.santaema.cl

Another Santa Ema white to be among this year's top wines (tasters found the reds too sweet and aggressive), this Sauvignon Blanc was met with mixed reactions, but those who loved it, *loved* it. Ultimately, it's hard to find much fault with this simple table wine. Its aromas and flavors are faint, so you have to concentrate to find what's lurking in the juice.

Nose At first, it may seem thin and vegetal. But stick your nose in deeper and you'll smell the lovely scents of white flowers and honeydew

Mouth It definitely comes on weak. There's a hint of a prickle, vague florality, some tropical fruits, and so-so acid. One blind taster thought it was a wimpy but inoffensive Pinot Grigio.

Design The green label against the pale, straw-colored wine is a nice effect. But the gold is a tacky touch to an otherwise classy bottle.

Santa Julia Cabernet Sauvignon

$11

Orgánica, Familia Zuccardi

Style Heavy New World red
Country Argentina **Vintage tasted** 2008
Grapes Cabernet Sauvignon
Drink with burgers, grilled mushrooms
Website www.familiazuccardi.com

It's hard not to like the sentiment behind proudly organic growers, even if they can occasionally seem preachy. This Argentine winery turns out a fruity, earthy wine that would be delicious even if it were loaded with chemicals. Like several of our picks from South America, this wine walks the classic Argentine line between New World and Old World styles, although its plush, sometimes jammy fruit pushes it a bit farther into New World territory.

Nose This wine is all about berries and earthy aromas. Some of our blind tasters felt that the fruit was so ripe-tasting as to be jammy.

Mouth Chocolate and strawberry jam dominate the mouth, with an underlying layer of bright, lively cherry flavors.

Design The unusually shaped label and simple black and white design make this bottle seem more expensive than it is, although we could have lived without the statue of a woman's head.

Santa Julia Chardonnay

Orgánica, Familia Zuccardi

Style Heavy New World white
Country Argentina **Vintage tasted** 2008
Grapes Chardonnay
Drink with clams, pastas with cream sauce
Website www.familiazuccardi.com

This organic Chardonnay is lively and fun to drink. Interestingly, the makers emphasize winemaking technique far more than land; while this attitude suggests a New World focus on winemaking over terroir, the wine itself is nicely balanced and marries New World fruit with Old World restraint.

Nose There's oak here, but it's not overwhelming. Citrus, pear, and a metallic aroma round out the wine.

Mouth It's admirably balanced, with enough steel to counter the oak.

Design Simple and sleek, this bottle looks like it should be on the wall of a trendy Manhattan apartment. We particularly love the minimalist logo and colored glass.

Santa Rita 120 Sauvignon Blanc $8

Style Light New World white
Country Chile **Vintage tasted** 2009
Grapes Sauvignon Blanc, Sémillon
Drink with pizza margherita, clam chowder
Website www.santarita.com

Two percent of this wine is actually made up of the Sémillon grape, a combination more common in Bordeaux than California. It may not seem like much, but even a small amount of a grape as different from Sauvignon Blanc as Sémillon can noticeably change the character of a wine. In this case, the result is a distinctly vegetal wine, with intense acidity and clean flavors.

Nose The bright aromas reminded our blind tasters of cooked greens and other vegetables.

Mouth It's wonderfully crisp, with intense acidity and a long finish. Our blind tasters were big fans.

Design We like the label design and the font of the large red "120," but something about the bottle itself struck us as cheap. Then again, it is—which is exactly why we like it.

Segura Viudas Brut Reserva

Two-time Wine Trials selection

$8

Style Sparkling
Country Spain **Vintage tasted** Non-Vintage
Grapes Macabeo, Parrellada, Xarel-lo
Drink with Szechuan dishes, crab cakes
Website www.seguraviudasusa.com

Great values are coming out of Spain, and Cavas are some of the best. They're sold for a fraction of the price of their similarly made French counterparts—and our blind tasters thought they were just as good, if not better. This is one of the cheapest versions on the market; despite being labeled a brut wine—and not containing a particularly high amount of sugar—it gives the impression of being slightly sweet.

Nose It has typical Cava apple aromas, but there's a hint of vanilla as well.

Mouth Strong bubbles and crisp acidity balance a profile that some tasters found a bit too sweet.

Design Cheaply gilded trim, muddy purples and maroons, and too many fonts, labels, logos, and coats of arms totally fail to create the image of royalty that Segura Viudas seems to have had in mind. No kings or queens here; this is strictly petty nobility.

Straccali Chianti

$10

Style Light Old World red
Country Italy **Vintage tasted** 2007
Grapes Sangiovese, Canaiolo, Merlot
Drink with prosciutto panini, spaghetti alla bolognese

The Italians have never been afraid to drink wines that are earthy or even dirty tasting, with scents of leaves, old books, or "barnyard." Centuries of experience have taught them that these are the wines that often go best with regional dishes—and that they are often delicious in their own right. This traditional-tasting Chianti embraces its heritage, providing complex, offbeat flavors that will pair beautifully with meaty pastas and other Tuscan dishes.

Nose The aggressive cherry is matched by a musty, almost dirty aroma that's strangely appealing.

Mouth It's well balanced, with a refreshing acidity that will help it match tomato sauces. The barnyard flavors linger.

Design The clichéd Tuscan landscape is less convincingly Italian than the wine itself, but at least the font is simple.

35° South Sauvignon Blanc

$9

Viña San Pedro Reserve • *Two-time selection*

Style Light New World white
Country Chile **Vintage tasted** 2008
Grapes Sauvignon Blanc
Drink with panini, mixed green salads, fried fish
Website www.sanpedro.cl

The Southern Hemisphere's 35th parallel isn't a bad place to grow grapes—especially Sauvignon Blanc. The finished product manages to take on that "cat pee" smell that so characterizes the grape. It's a repulsive image, but the description works; otherwise, we can't think of a better way to describe the aromas than, "uh, smells like Sauvignon Blanc." It's one of the most distinct aromatic profiles in the wine world, and for the second year in a row, this *Wine Trials* honoree has it in spades.

Nose It's got loads of fresh green apple and pear.

Mouth There's no missing that this is a Sauvignon Blanc—if the cat pee aroma doesn't tip you off, the intense, vibrant acidity will.

Design The label manages to pull off a navigational theme, borrowing from the look of old maps, without coming off as too precious or gimmicky. Bright touches of orange lighten things up.

337 Red
DFV Wines

$15

Style Heavy New World red
Country California **Vintage tasted** 2007
Grapes Cabernet Sauvignon
Drink with chili, lentil soup

This wine is named after the clone of the Cabernet grape that composes it, and we have to respect anyone who's enough of a wine wonk to put a clone number on a bottle. For those who aren't in the know, a clone is like a breed of a particular wine grape. This wine is advertised as the best of both worlds: a restrained French grape clone grown under the hot California sun. That seems like wishful thinking, though, as this wine is as powerful, extracted, and thoroughly New World as it could possibly be.

Nose There's a lot to love here: cola, cherry, heavy fruit, and a rich "forest" smell all compete for attention.

Mouth It's dark and tannic, with a smooth layer of chocolate flavors.

Design The label looks like the title screen for a campy horror film. We really wish Cabs would ease up on the red-and-black color scheme, but at least we'll have plenty of choices for wines to drink on Halloween.

Trackers Crossing Cabernet Sauvignon $8

Style Heavy New World red
Country Australia **Vintage tasted** 2007
Grapes Cabernet Sauvignon
Drink with juicy steaks, beef with red wine sauces

The Australians believe in going big or going home, and this wine really goes big. No one can accuse the makers of this chock-full-of-spice-berries-and-oak wine of being too timid. And while some might complain that the wine lacks restraint, there's something refreshing about just cutting the brakes and pushing winemaking possibilities to the edge. We don't recommend this wine as an everyday staple, but when you need excitement and power, this is a good place to start.

Nose It's got an aggressive nose, led by mulled spice and berries.

Mouth As one blind taster said, it tastes like it smells: heavy, oaky, and rich with blackberry and vanilla.

Design We're a bit too tired of Australian wines with kangaroos on the front to give this bottle a fair shake, but we think the cluttered design and three different labels on the front would have called the look into question anyway.

Trapiche Malbec

Two-time Wine Trials selection

$9

Style Heavy New World red
Country Argentina **Vintage tasted** 2008
Grapes Malbec
Drink with blood sausage, grilled steak, sweetbreads
Website www.trapiche.com.ar

This big, full Argentine wine—and two-time *Wine Trials* honoree—has bold tannins and noticeable acidity, making it a bit challenging to drink on its own. But pair it with food, especially a hearty steak, and you'll have some delicious results. The protein tames the tannin, leaving the wine with just enough roughness to stand up to the meat. The end result is a happy marriage of juicy flavors and texture.

Nose It's fruit-forward, with lots of ripe berries. But our blind tasters also found hints of coffee, chocolate, nuts, and pepper.

Mouth It's fairly acidic and a bit unbalanced in the mouth. But as we said, pairing it with a juicy steak will fix all faults.

Design This bottle is far better than last year's. Elegant white space has replaced the clichéd vineyard landscape, and even the eagle looks more stylish. Thankfully, they preserved the heavy, tapered bottle that we loved so much.

Trapiche Cabernet Sauvignon

$11

Oak Cask (Roble)

Style Heavy New World red
Country Argentina **Vintage tasted** 2007
Grapes Cabernet Sauvignon
Drink with grilled sirloin, beef stew
Website www.trapiche.com.ar

This is a powerful Cabernet Sauvignon, not unlike the two-time *Wine Trials* favorite Trapiche Malbec. Many Argentine Cabernets occupy a happy medium between Australian fruit bombs and more restrained Old World efforts; this wine certainly leans towards ripe fruit flavors, but it has enough structure and subtlety to go well with food. It's in the "Roble" series—oak-aged—but the oak doesn't dominate this flavor profile.

Nose There's lots of ripe red cherry, along with plum and vanilla. One blind taster also identified a hint of hay.

Mouth It's big and tannic in the mouth—definitely an old-fashioned meat wine.

Design This is the same design we objected to last year: we don't mind the mountainous landscape and soaring bird, but its placement beneath all the text seems incoherent. We're big fans of the bottle itself, though.

Twin Vines Vinho Verde

Fonseca

$7

BARGAIN

Style Light Old World white
Country Portugal **Vintage tasted** 2008
Grapes Loureiro, Trajadura, Pedernã, Alvarinho
Drink with soft-shell crab, pasta salad
Website www.jmf.pt

With its pleasing fruit and citrus flavors, mouthwatering acidity, and shockingly low price tag, it's a mystery why Vinho Verde isn't served on every porch in America. Whatever the issue, we're happy to see that these Portuguese wines are slowly catching on. This bottle is a perfect example of the classic Vinho Verde style, and we recommend it with shellfish or as a party wine.

Nose The aromas are peachy, with heavy notes of pear and apple.

Mouth Intense apple flavors continue, matched by bracing acidity and the slight prickle characteristic of Vinho Verde. As several of our blind tasters noted, this is a perfect summer wine.

Design "Busy" doesn't begin to describe what's going on here. The color scheme is nice, but the exploding tangle of vines looks like it's in need of some serious pruning.

Vida Orgánica Malbec

$9

Familia Zuccardi • *Two-time Wine Trials selection*

Style Heavy New World red
Country Argentina **Vintage tasted** 2008
Grapes Malbec
Drink with grilled lamb, chorizo

Argentine Malbecs are usually a safe bet for value: the combination of an easy-to-like grape, ideal growing conditions, a country without the name recognition of France or Italy, and importers who tend to pick decent wines, produces offerings that are a comfortable refuge on a restaurant wine list. With its rich flavors, pleasant fruit, and food-friendly structure, this impressively inexpensive wine is no exception to the Malbec rule. And Familia Zuccardi's devotion to organic growing means you can feel good about yourself when you pour a glass.

Nose Our blind tasters loved the full chocolate and blueberry aromas.

Mouth It's less fruity than might be expected, with chocolate, spice, and herbal flavors. There are also some nice tannins, making it an ideal match for meat.

Design The beautiful paper looks nicely aged, and the font seems like it might actually be written by a human being.

Villa Maria Sauvignon Blanc

$15

Private Bin • *Two-time Wine Trials selection*

Style Light New World white
Country New Zealand **Vintage tasted** 2008
Grapes Sauvignon Blanc
Drink with whole roasted fish, shrimp cocktail
Website www.villamaria.co.nz

Despite a name that's about as evocative of New Zealand as a baked tortilla, this wine is a classic Kiwi concoction. We are also impressed with the makers' unabashed commitment to screw tops: Villa Maria, to achieve better consistency, was the first maker in the world to declare its winery a "cork-free zone."

Nose Like the previous vintage, which appeared in the first edition of *The Wine Trials*, this wine has classic Sauvignon Blanc aromas of grapefruit, lime, and grass.

Mouth A slight prickle on the tongue and sharp acidity round out the list of classic New Zealand characteristics.

Design There's really no excuse for a New World winery founded in 1961 to have a coat of arms. We wish Villa Maria would cut out the faux-aristocratic red and gold and create a bottle that reflects the fun, lively wine inside.

Vitiano

Falesco, Umbria IGT • *Two-time Wine Trials selection*

$9

Style Light Old World red
Country Italy **Vintage tasted** 2006
Grapes Cabernet Sauvignon, Merlot, Sangiovese
Drink with braised beef, vegetable stew
Website www.falesco.it

This two-time *Wine Trials* honoree might be called a "Super-Umbrian," as it mimics the Tuscan producers' newly acquired habit of blending Cabernet Sauvignon and/or Merlot with local grape varieties to make "Super-Tuscans." Umbria is Tuscany's neighbor, equally beautiful but less heralded by wine and travel magazines. This wine shares the Super-Tuscan propensity for big, New World flavors designed to appeal to the Robert Parkers of the world.

Nose It's certainly unique—our blind tasters picked up on everything from blueberry cordial to coffee, although a few tasters found the nose too chemical.

Mouth There's a strong oak influence, but the wine remains fairly balanced. One blind taster favorably compared it to candy and dirt.

Design It's not bad, it's just sad: the grapes are now enumerated right on the front of the bottle, in accordance with New World labeling convention. We lament the death of tradition.

Appendix Conclusions of the 2008 experiment

By Johan Almenberg and Anna Dreber Almenberg

Contrary to what we might expect, when they are unaware of the price, people do not appreciate expensive wines more than cheap wines. In a sample of more than 6,000 blind tastings, we find that the correlation between price and overall rating is small and *negative*, suggesting that individuals on average enjoy more expensive wines slightly *less*. For people with wine training ("experts"), however, we find indications of a positive correlation.

In the regression analysis, the dependent variable is the overall rating, measured on a scale from 1 to 4, with 4 being the highest rating. The price variable is the natural logarithm of the dollar price. (If we didn't do this, we would be expecting a one-dollar increase to have the same effect at the $5 price level as at the $50 price level; this seems counterintuitive. We do get the same qualitative results using the dollar prices, but the statistical significance of the coefficients deteriorates.)

We use an ordered probit estimator as well as a linear estimator (OLS). In both cases we use robust standard errors. The ordered probit estimator is particularly well suited to an ordinal dependent variable, but we find that OLS also performs well, and yields estimates that are easier to interpret. In any case, the two models generate highly consistent results.

We employ three model specifications, and run all three using both the ordered probit and the OLS estimator. In Model 1, we regress the overall rating assigned to wine i, by individual j, on the price of the wine. In Model 2, we allow for the possibility that wine "experts," such as sommeliers or people with professional wine training, rate wines in a different manner. We include a dummy variable for being an expert, as well as an interaction term for price and the expert dummy. In a linear regression, this allows both the intercept and the slope coefficient to differ for experts and non-experts. In terms of the linear model, we can write these two models as

$$(1) \ y_i = \beta_0 + \beta_1 \ln(PRICE_i) + \varepsilon_i$$

and

$$(2) \ y_i = \beta_0 + \beta_1 \ln(PRICE_i) + \beta_2 EXPERT_j + \beta_3 \ln(PRICE_i) * EXPERT_j + \varepsilon_i$$

If individuals found that more expensive wine tasted better, the correlation between overall rating and price would be positive. In our sample, this is not the case: the coefficient on price is *negative* regardless of whether we use ordered probit or OLS. The linear estimator offers an interpretation of the magnitude of the effect: when we estimate model 1 using OLS, the coefficient is about -0.04, implying that a 100% increase in the (natural) log of the price is associated with a 0.04 reduction in the overall rating. The negative effect is moderate, but statistically significant (*p*-value: 0.038).

Unlike the non-experts, experts assign as high, or higher, ratings to more expensive wines. The interaction term for price and being an expert is highly statistically significant throughout. Controlling for experts produces a larger negative effect of price for non-experts, with improved statistical significance (ordered probit/OLS *p*-values: 0.013/0.012).

In addition, experts assign overall ratings that are on average half a rating point lower (OLS coefficient on the expert dummy: -0.448, *p*-value < 0.001). Regardless of whether we use ordered probit or OLS, estimation of Model 2 indicates that the correlation between price and overall rating is positive—or, at any rate, non-negative—

for experts. The "net" coefficient for experts is the sum of the coefficient on ln(price) and the coefficient on ln(price)*expert. With OLS, this is approximately 0.1 and marginally statistically significant (p-value: 0.09). For ordered probit, the net coefficient is about 0.11 and marginally statistically significant (p-value: 0.099). The price coefficient for non-experts is negative.

When we estimate Model 2 using OLS, the model predicts that for a wine that costs ten times more than another wine, if we were to use a 100-point scale (such as that used by *Wine Spectator*), the linear model predicts that for a wine that costs 10 times more than another wine, non-experts will on average assign an overall rating that is about four points *lower*, whereas experts will assign an overall rating that is about seven points *higher*. If the dollar price increases by a factor of 10, ln(price) increases by about 2.3. Hence the predicted effect on the overall rating of tenfold increase in the dollar price is 2.3 times the ln(price) coefficient for non-experts and experts, respectively.

We also test a third model, including individual fixed effects. Model 3 is essentially the same as Model 2, except that we add a dummy variable j for each individual taster. Including the fixed effects does not affect the qualitative results, and the coefficients themselves change only slightly. A Wald test rejects that the fixed effects are jointly equal to zero, by a wide margin (p-value < 0.001). All of these results apply regardless of whether we use ordered probit or OLS.

To make sure that our results are not driven by wines at the extreme ends of the price range, we also run our regressions on a reduced sample, omitting observations in the top and bottom deciles of the price distribution. Given the broad range of prices in the sample, this is an appropriate precaution. The wines in the reduced sample range in price from $6 to $15.

Using the reduced sample, we estimate Model 2 using both ordered probit and OLS, in each case with and without fixed effects. The qualitative results are highly consistent with those we get when using the full sample. In fact, the effects are larger, and the statistical significance improves further (p-value, non-expert price coefficient: 0.001).

Index of wines

Notes